HARVEY "SMOKEY" DANIELS

with sketchnotes by **Tanny McGregor**

The Curious

10 Structures for Teaching with Student-Directed Inquiry

Classroom

HEINEMANN
Portsmouth, NH

Heinemann
361 Hanover Street
Portsmouth, NH 03801–3912
www.heinemann.com

Offices and agents throughout the world

The author and publisher wish to thank those who have generously given permission to reprint borrowed material:

Inquiry Approach Versus Coverage Approach: From *Comprehension and Collaboration: Inquiry Circles in Action* by Stephanie Harvey and Harvey Daniels. Copyright © 2009 by Stephanie Harvey and Harvey Daniels. Published by Heinemann, Portsmouth, NH. All rights reserved. Heinemann currently publishes a second edition of *Comprehension and Collaboration*.

Acknowledgments for borrowed material continue on p. 198.

Library of Congress Cataloging-in-Publication Data
Name: Daniels, Harvey, author.
Title: The curious classroom : 10 structures for teaching with student-directed inquiry / Harvey "Smokey" Daniels with Sketchnotes by Tanny McGregor.
Description: Portsmouth, NH : Heinemann, [2017] | Includes bibliographic references.
Identifiers: LCCN 2016054400 | ISBN 9780325089904
Subjects: LCSH: Inquiry-based learning. | Student-centered learning.
Classification: LCC LB1027.23 .D38 2017 | DDC 371.39—dc23

LC record available at https://lccn.loc.gov/2016054400

Editor: Tobey Antao
Production: Vicki Kasabian
Interior design: Suzanne Heiser
Cover design: Lisa A. Fowler
Cover photograph: Alyssa Zaffiro
Typesetter: Kim Arney
Manufacturing: Steve Bernier

Printed in the United States of America on acid-free paper
21 20 19   VP   3 4 5

Contents

What is inquiry? It's building instruction out of children's curiosity, rather than from a textbook. It's an active, lively classroom where children make choices and take responsibility for their learning. It's backed by research, and it promotes deep student engagement.

1 Demonstrate Your Own Curiosity   2

In our inquiry classrooms, we are less frequently playing the boss/expert role. Instead, we are acting more like a lead learner, a coach, a facilitator, or, some days, a research assistant. Today's students urgently need to see as many thoughtful, curious, resourceful, and critical adults as they can. So we model our own curious lives for kids.

Models in this chapter:

2 Investigate Ourselves and Our Classmates   20

Doing genuine inquiry work requires kids to rely on every classmate as a potential partner, co-investigator, or audience for the topic they are pursuing. If you want a curious, collaborative, inquiry-ready classroom, then you are in the friendship-creating business.

Models in this chapter:

3 Capture and Honor Kids' Questions 42

If we are going to build our instruction out of kids' questions—whether these are about a required curriculum or whether they emerge from children's free-range curiosity—we need a system. To create a culture of questioning and investigation, we need to solicit and record topics kids wonder about, make time for them, pursue them, and keep track of kids' efforts along the way.

Models in this chapter:

4 Begin the Day with Soft Starts 58

Soft starts are an investment in the rest of the day. If kids begin the morning by exercising their own curiosity, under their own control, they are more likely to be responsible and curious all day long.

Models in this chapter:

5 Check Our News Feed 78

Not only can the news stimulate inquiry projects of all sorts, it also sets children on a path to becoming active, aware, and critical citizens of their communities and of the world.

Models in this chapter:

6 Hang Out with an Expert 98

By spending time with experts, kids learn authentic and reliable information and also witness what passionate and sustained devotion to a specialty looks like. You'd be amazed by how many busy professionals will happily take half a day off to come to your school and talk to a room full of nine-year-olds about their work.

Models in this chapter:

7 Pursue Kids' Own Questions with Mini-Inquiries 120

Children come up with questions that are more profound, more interesting, and sometimes, more charmingly original than we grown-ups would ever think of. When we turn the classroom over to kid-driven inquiry, students see the real, messy process of "finding out," and how exciting it is. And they can't help falling in love with it.

Models in this chapter:

8 Address Curricular Units with Mini-Inquiries   140

When we flip on the "curiosity switch" in the brains of our students, we empower them to grapple, persist, and build knowledge on topics they would never have chosen on their own.

Models in this chapter:

9 Lean into a Crisis 152

Crises, small and large, happen in our classrooms every year. We react to these events first from our hearts, and then by using inquiry strategies to help kids cope, build understanding, and carry on in hope.

Models in this chapter:

10 Learn with Partners and Pioneers 174

As we teachers grow in our inquiry practice, we need allies. We need models of how to reach out to colleagues, principals, parents, and our district leaders. We can get such practical advice from schools that have become inquiry pioneers.

Models in this chapter:

Contributing Educators

Hayley Abell

Sara Ahmed

Amber Ankrom

Daniel Argyres

Patrice Ball

Kathy Bartlemay

Katie Block

Brad Buhrow

Elaine Cameron

Elaine Daniels

Megan Dixon

Julie Eisenhauer

Lisa Elliott

Annie Gentithes

Jessica Gonzalez-Boe

Heather Green

Tery Gunter

Carolynn Klein Hageman

Stacy Hansen

Mary Beth Hes

Heather Isham

Beth Kaminski

Christina Jepsen

Amy Lau

Lindsay Law

Jessica Lenz

Ali Locker

Tanny McGregor

Debbie McLachlan

Charity Meyer

Claudia Michelman

Meghan Morris

Brian Murphy

Jenny Murray

Sue Musson

Steve Newcomer

Darcy Nidey

Ashley Ohmstede

Laura Olson

Lyndsey Popham

Clint Prohaska

Michelle Reich

Kari Ridolfi

Joyce Sanchez

Abby Schmitz

Micki Schumacher

Faith Shellabarger

Sarah Van Lieshout

Becca Woolridge

Deb Zaffiro

Kristin Ziemke

Partner Schools

Glenwood Elementary School, Greenfield, Wisconsin

Eason Elementary School, Waukee, Iowa

Duke School, Durham, North Carolina

Contributing Schools

Burley School, Chicago, Illinois

Big Shoulders Foundation, Chicago, Illinois

Virginia Chance School, Louisville, Kentucky

The Bishop's School, La Jolla, California

Disney 2 Magnet School, Chicago, Illinois

Santa Fe Community College, Santa Fe, New Mexico

Tesuque Owingeh Pueblo School, Tesuque, New Mexico

Withamsville-Tobasco Elementary, Withamsville, Ohio

Acknowledgments

This is something like my twentieth book, depending on how you count second editions. This one has more people to thank than any of its predecessors. Time to break out the huzzahs! Heartfelt salutes to:

The partner schools, Glenwood, Eason, and Duke. The happiest year of my professional life was spent in your classrooms, capturing your stories of instructional excellence.

The contributing teachers and schools. We've had a variety of relationships, some reaching back decades. I appreciate your trust in sharing your thinking with me and our readers.

The multiarticle contributors: Beth, Megan, Sarah V, Laura, Faith, Kari, Ashley, Katie, and Sara A. You are now qualified to write your own books!

Deb Zaffiro: Not only is she the World's Greatest Coach, Deb has also been my ally, confidante, sounding board, research guru, and cheerleader through this whole project. Love you, my friend.

Our ace photographers, Alyssa Zaffiro, Ali Locker, Kathy Bartlemay, and those DIY teachers who shot their own.

Tanny McGregor for her glorious sketchnotes, which provide a creative conclusion to every chapter.

Heinemann: I am celebrating my thirty-second anniversary with the premier publisher in our field. I never cease to be amazed by Heinemann's astonishing team, where every member is at the top of their game. A hearty New Mexico *muchas gracias* to Vicki Boyd, Lisa Fowler, Stephen Perepeluk, Patty Adams, Vicki Kasabian, Eric Chalek, Brett Whitmarsh, Sarah Fournier, Suzanne Heiser, Sarah Weaver, Amanda Bondi, Sherry Day, Michael Grover, and everyone else under the roof. Eternal gratitude to the PD team—Mim Easton, Michelle Flynn, Cheryl Savage, Maureen Foster, Cherie Bartlett, Heidi Perham, Cathy Brophy, and Donna Robillard, who handle my speaking dates with gusto and patience.

My editor: Tobey Antao has been my editor for a whole string of books now. She is one of the smartest people I've ever met, including me. She does the things all great editors do—helps me shape chaotic ideas, finds my dumb mistakes, and insinuates her graceful wording when my text clunks—all the while making me think it was my idea. She is a skilled manager of outsized egos, and we playfully argue a lot about who is the wisest: you are; no, you are; no, *you* are. We have fun doing this work. But Tobey also has serious skin in the game. Matilda, her six-year-old daughter, is starting her journey through the public schools. Needless to say, Tilda is adorable, and more important, she's *precious,* as all children in this country are. I want Tilda's life to bring her into schools like the ones in this book, where smart and caring teachers evoke her curiosity, honor her questions, guide her into a lifetime of self-directed inquiry—and just love her to pieces.

My writing mentors: My personal reading workshop starts every morning around 5:30 a.m. and runs for an hour or two. This is my personal study hall, where I apprentice myself to my favorite nonfiction writers in the world: Barbara Ehrenreich, Matt Taibbi, James Wolcott, Jelani Cobb, Jon Krakauer, Erik Larson, Michael Lewis, Naomi Klein, Dave Eggers, Ta-Nehisi Coates, Amy Davidson, George Packer (well, basically everyone at the *New Yorker*), and my Santa Fe neighbor Hampton Sides.

The Fam: My son, Nick, was five years old and my daughter, Marny, was unborn when I published my first book. Now, they are thirty-eight and thirty-two. They've probably answered people a few thousand times by saying, "Uh, my dad writes books," but have never had the chance to point those curious friends toward the *New York Times* best-seller list. Sorry about that, guys; teacher books only.

Nick's and Marny's school experiences—the good, the bad, and the ugly—have animated every one of my books. I write to create conditions such that all students have more of the good times my kids encountered, and fewer of the rigid structures and kid-unfriendly programs they sometimes suffered through.

Elaine and I have been parenting and coteaching all this time. Now that the kids are de-nested, our idea of fun is to plan out an inquiry project for her community college class *and* a parallel one for me to use in a teacher workshop. Then I fly home from wherever, and we compare notes. Elaine is also my first teacher about classroom community, empathy, and the role of love in teaching. When you see her with students, you witness a human being who's all in, completely authentic, and freely available to the persons and the moment. Being married to her is a flow-state experience.

Introduction

Welcome to Student-Directed Inquiry

This is a book about teaching with inquiry, which means building instruction out of children's curiosity, rather than from a curriculum guide, a standard textbook, or a handed-down unit. It means kids investigating and exploring, instead of just sitting and listening. It means an active, lively space where children make choices and take responsibility for their learning. It means classrooms where teachers flow between their role as an expert and their job as lead learner and facilitator of research. Inquiry means children partner up to gather information, build knowledge, and then teach the world, together.

Inquiry is an exciting and energizing way to engage kids' hearts and minds—*and* to cover content and meet standards. It holds important rewards for our students and delight for the adults working with them. But inquiry also requires some courage and some adjustments from us. The two biggest questions I hear from teachers are:

1. How do you find the *time* to try out kid-driven inquiries? I have my hands full trying to cover the official curriculum.

2. What are some quick and safe *structures* for getting started? I want to start small, dip my toe in the water, see how it works, and make sure my kids can handle it.

Glenwood students kept a timeline of an eagle family from first eggs to spring fledgling.

The next two hundred pages address those concerns with specific and practical strategies, lessons, and models. Together, we will work our way up a ladder of student-directed learning that shows how to make room for inquiry in our schedules and to use that time well. By the end of this book, after you have tried out some of its ten major structures, I hope you will say two things:

"I never knew my kids were capable of working at this level."

and

"This is the most fun I have ever had in my teaching life."

But to begin, let's visit a classroom where inquiry is already in progress.

On this warm spring day, I am visiting Eason Elementary School, just west of Des Moines, Iowa. I step into Micki Schumacher's colorful first-grade room, where the kids are in the middle of "mini-inquiry" research projects on topics of their choice. A few minutes ago, Micki modeled how she pursues a curiosity question of her own ("Is our school in 'Tornado Alley,' and what does that mean?"). Then, on a big chart, she scribed a list of questions suggested by the kids.

Now the kids have been released to research their own questions, using laptops, their Wonder Notebooks, and a partner, if they want one.

I circulate through the room, sitting in briefly with kids who are investigating questions like these:

- Why do zebras have strips [stripes]?
- Who is puntsutawney [Punxsutawney] Phil?
- How can you make someoun's [someone's] day?
- How do animals communicate?
- How are gummy bars [bears] made?
- What causes a shooting star?
- Why isn's evering [isn't everything] free?

When I come over to Jenita and Audrey, I see their topic neatly typed on the laptop in front of them: "Why is Pluto no longer a planet?" As an astronomy enthusiast myself, I tuck in to hear what they're up to.

As with almost every other activity in this book, laptops or tablets are not *required*. Jenita and Audrey could just as well have jotted notes about their Pluto inquiry on paper. But when a piece of technology really amplifies the learning, I'll mention it for consideration.

POINT OUT

The girls are looking at a Kids Discover page that explains how Pluto was demoted from planethood for not being big enough. The problem was that other, significantly larger objects had been detected beyond Pluto's orbit. During a lull in the conversation, Audrey looks at me as if I am supposed to contribute something.

"I am really interested in the solar system, too," I offer. "In fact, I just read an amazing article in a magazine called *Scientific American* that says there might be another big planet in our solar system that we haven't even discovered yet. The astronomers are calling it Planet X."

The kids seem interested, so I add, "They think it would be a lot like Earth, with a rocky surface and maybe a little bigger. But much further out from the sun." Lucy and Avery, two girls working across the table, have now looked up from their screens to listen in. At this point, Jenita turns to me thoughtfully and asks: "How did the universe begin, anyway?"

Jenita asks some big questions.

My mind is going: "This is the greatest question I have ever heard from a first grader." But outwardly, I demur, saying something like, "No one is completely sure. Scientists have been working on this for centuries. We'd all be famous if we could settle the debate."

Now all four girls stare at me with a look that says: "We haven't got all day, man; what's the deal?"

So I launch into the Big Bang theory. I explain that we can infer there was an initiating explosion because astronomers have shown that the universe is still expanding outward. I pause to ask, "Do you guys know what *infer* means?" Jenita just nods and says, "Sure, we infer every day in here."

The kids lean in as I dive deeper into the concept of an ever-expanding universe. I catch myself and laugh. "You know, we are doing college-level physics right now." No one but me seems to find this particularly noteworthy.

Something that fascinates me, as a teacher of many decades, is that I have finally found a moment in which *giving information* can be an effective teaching method: when kids have chosen their own research topic, dug deeply into it, and then run up against an information deficit. This is the mother of all teachable moments.

These six-year-olds seem to be in a "flow state." They are hanging on my every word. They listen as if I am recounting a trip to Disney World.

Looking back a few weeks later, I'm not sure how much astrophysics Jenita, Audrey, Lucy, and Avery remember from our time together. But I do know this: those girls were seized by curiosity, hungry to build knowledge, and fully in charge of their own learning. And those experiences, those *habits of mind*, will serve them for the rest of their lives.

These lucky kids are attending an inquiry school in a district that has committed itself to honoring kids' questions and teaching them how to find answers for themselves. Every morning, Eason's children roll off the bus brimming with wonders—and eager to put their adults to work helping them investigate the burning questions that surge through their minds. Over in the teachers' parking lot are more smiling faces, the school's "lead learners" toting in armloads of books, rolled-up charts, bulging book bags, random props, and, balanced in there somehow, drippy Starbucks cups.

Realities

Before we get too starry-eyed here, let's check some facts. The teachers at Eason School have a mandated curriculum, standardized tests, and district-adopted programs to deal with, just like the rest of us. They don't necessarily have wizard-level technology or bulging bookrooms. And they are just as likely to have thirty kids—each with his or her own perspectives, needs, and strengths—as we are.

What's different is that they have flipped their thinking. Where these educators used to worry about covering the material, they now plan how to evoke kids' curiosity. When they once focused on assigning and assessing finished products, they now teach *thinking*: problem posing, researching, vetting, corroborating, analyzing, criticizing, and presenting. They have two watchwords:

1. Honor kids' own questions.

2. Make the required curriculum into questions kids can't resist investigating.

This casual-sounding "flip" wasn't easy here at Eason, or at Glenwood, Duke, Burley, or any of the other schools we'll visit in this book. They all started small. They sure didn't plunge directly into full-scale, year-round inquiry units.

Instead, these teachers began with short, well-structured lessons that they used to test the kids' capabilities—and their own comfort level—with inquiry. And before they even took that first step, they *subtracted* something from their day. For example, if a teacher had a standard morning "bellringer/worksheet" regime, she'd suspend it for a while to make time to experiment with inquiry.

Many set the stage by giving five-minute lessons during which they shared their own curious lives with kids, modeling how they had hunted down the answers they sought. This could be as simple as telling about a book or article they had read, or more complex, such as sharing a personal investigation they were undertaking outside school. Megan Dixon had her second graders transfixed for weeks over her growing family's agonizing decision whether to buy a minivan and thus become "uncool forever."

Other teachers dipped a toe in the water by opening their mornings with "soft starts," swapping fifteen minutes of whole-class teaching for a quiet time when each student could choose something to learn about. When they saw that kids could handle that freedom, they set up wonder walls to capture and honor students' questions, returning to them for a few minutes later in the day or the week.

As kids proved their trustworthiness and teachers gained confidence, they tried longer and more complex inquiry structures. They found that if they set up a weekly Genius Hour, students were not just exercising their own need to know, but also covering heaps of standards along the way. Whatever topic they had chosen, kids were closely reading nonfiction text; conducting web research from reliable sources; working in collaborative teams; having respectful debates with classmates; and representing their thinking in writing, drawing, and speech.

When big, required curricular units came along, teachers would first ask kids: "What questions do you have about _____?" (e.g., insects, weather, community helpers, native peoples, Wisconsin history, and so on). They would build the instruction around kids' questions, which, lo and behold, usually covered and exceeded the official learning targets. And, as kids repeatedly demonstrated their capability, teachers felt comfortable to build more and more inquiry into their calendars.

As teachers became more fluent with inquiry, and their students mastered its procedures, these classroom communities could better handle the problems and crises that invariably come up over the span of a school year: a class pet dies, a classmate has a house fire, there is scary news on TV. As inquiry-ready kids, they could not only discuss and examine an issue but also turn to action: building awareness, advocating, or offering comfort and aid.

The Inquiry Trend

As I write this, the moment is auspicious for inquiry and curiosity. After a decade or three (depending how you count) of test-driven, data-obsessed school reform, we are enjoying a course correction. More flexibility and choice have returned to the states with the 2015 signing of the Every Student Succeeds Act. Working with teachers and schools in nineteen states this year, I have been hearing big sighs of relief as teachers feel the gradual return of their professional autonomy in the classroom.

Several ongoing conversations in education today combine to favor the development of more inquiry-based, curiosity-driven teaching.

Factors That Favor Inquiry Teaching

Research on Curiosity and Interest

Our teacher guts have always told us that kids learn more when they are curious about or interested in a subject. Now, a slew of brain research validates our instinct. Studies show that curiosity is a measurable mind-state during which learners not only hoover up information about a topic, but will also remember extraneous or accompanying events. In other words, we seem to have a "curiosity switch" that, when flipped, can juice up powerful learning (Strauss 2012).

> **Takeaway: Inquiry activates kids' curiosity.**

Creativity and Innovation

Ask anyone from another country what makes America different and they'll usually answer that it's our innovation or our creativity. We Americans think differently—sometimes in very valuable ways. Unfortunately, with its obsessive focus on math and reading test scores, our recent cycle of school reform inadvertently suppressed the development of our number one national asset. The business world is already addressing this creativity gap and generating ways to better nurture original thinking. Daniel Pink's work is all about tapping people's intrinsic motivation to unleash innovative ideas and to enhance organizations (2009). Emma Seppala's research at Stanford offers a formula for making time, room, and space for unpressured creative thinking, both at work and in schools (2016).

> **Takeaway: Inquiry unleashes children's creativity.**

Available Models

There is a fast-developing world of structures, tools, and materials that support inquiry teaching. The Buck Institute's Project-Based Learning continues to offer the field useful publications, events, and models (2016). Expeditionary Learning (now called ELS) has grown quickly in recent years, but maintained its principle of helping kids "have wonderful ideas" (2015). Responsive Classroom offers high-quality support for the collaboration and climate that inquiry classrooms require (2016). Our own research group has specialized in student-driven, rather than teacher-planned, inquiry units (Harvey and Daniels 2015; Daniels and Ahmed 2015; Daniels and Steineke 2014).

> **Takeaway: We now have plenty of tools and supports for inquiry teaching.**

Technology

Visiting schools these days, it sometimes feels like a technology festival. Symbaloo, Padlet, Kiddle, Edmodo, Google Classroom—and those are just the old ones! After decades of unfulfilled promises, an age of truly powerful tech-enabled learning is finally upon us. Today, kids can do things that were never possible before, reaching out to the world to investigate, build knowledge, and teach others. As these new tools and platforms are introduced, teachers are skillfully differentiating between the steak and the sizzle, focusing on the apps that aren't just gimmicks, but that genuinely amplify good teaching (Muhtaris and Ziemke 2015).

> **Takeaway: Inquiry gives kids a real purpose for using the latest technology.**

Work World Ideas

The business community is always a source of ideas for schools, from the assembly-line model that we are still trying to outgrow, to some more promising ideas circulating today. Google's now sadly abandoned policy of giving employees one full day a week to pursue their own projects has spurred a school version we often call Genius Hour (Kessler 2013). And today's more progressive STEM programs, the ones that emphasize play, doing, trial and error, teaming, risk taking, and real-world applications, are feeding useful ideas to inquiry-based learning.

> **Takeaway: Inquiry learning parallels the workplace innovations and procedures.**

Climate and Collaboration

We have an acute recognition that bullying, discrimination, and violence too often mar our school communities. Now serious action steps and alternatives are being developed and disseminated. There is an urgent recognition that we can (and must) explicitly teach friendliness, empathy, collaboration, and social-academic skills (Daniels and Steineke 2014).

> **Takeaway: Inquiry provides social-emotional learning through teamwork, empathy, and shared responsibility.**

Engagement

Sometimes school is boring. This is not news to students, but the adults seem to have just gotten the message. Suddenly there is talk everywhere about student engagement. Bill Gates is even researching galvanic skin response bracelets (using essentially the same technology as mood rings) that could monitor kids' "engagement" in class (Strauss 2012). On the more hopeful side, researchers are showing that "engaged" doesn't necessarily mean *happy*. Students may tackle certain work out of mere compliance or under coercion, but this is not the same self-sustaining dynamic that curiosity offers. The questions now under debate: Are we setting too low a standard for kids' frame of mind in school? Should we be talking not just about obedience, but about joy, passion, play, fun, flow, and awe (Seppala 2016)?

> **Takeaway: Inquiry makes school feel worthwhile.**

Social-Academic Skills

We are having a great debate about student motivation, self-regulation, and persistence. It is often argued that students, especially those from poor, urban, and minority communities, fail in school because they lack "grit," defined as a passion for long-term goals combined with strict self-discipline. Others argue that this exculpates the school by placing the blame on the student. Grit is not a character trait, they argue, but more an aspect of the tasks you are asked to do. If you are required to gut and clean a thousand fish every day (or do a hundred odd-numbered math problems as homework), a little grit might well come in handy. But kids who face the challenges of poverty, of systemic racism, or of inner-city urban life prove that they have grit just by getting to school every day. Students show motivation in class when the work is interesting and worth doing.

Takeaway: Inquiry promotes children's effort and persistence.

Heritage and Research

Inquiry learning is no fad. It has a deep history of research and practice in American education. The century-old contributions of John Dewey and William Kirkpatrick built a strong foundation, but other key contributions have come over the past seventy years. Spurred by development of constructivist learning theory and social psychology, the discovery learning movement was born in the 1960s, led by figures like Jerome Bruner. A breakthrough finding of this research was that traditional learning theories could not explain how children learned their native language. Normally developing children invent language structures *they have never heard from adults*: Daddy goed to work, I have two feets, and so on. This showed us that learners don't just receive but actively construct knowledge by sampling and actively manipulating the information around them. Not surprisingly, given a hundred years of such study, we can now document improved academic achievement in a variety of settings and grade levels where inquiry-based approaches are in place (Buck Institute 2016).

Takeaway: Inquiry has a cohesive learning theory and a strong evidence base.

Try This

Stop reading this book for a moment (I know that will be painful, right?) and think back to a time you were really curious about something. This could be during your childhood, outside of school, or today in your adult life. Use these "symptoms" of curiosity to help you locate such an experience in your own life.

Felt energized
Got totally involved
Lost track of time
Was highly focused
Couldn't be distracted
Stuck to it
Found extra time to pursue it
Felt pleasure or delight
Kept having more questions
Remembered what you learned
Later shared your learning with others

Got one? Great. Now consider these questions. If you are reading this book with a study group, by all means discuss them out loud.

What was the topic or activity?
How did you get hooked?
Where did this happen?
Was anyone else involved as a mentor or partner?
How did you feel emotionally?
How would you describe your state of mind?

As you recollect these conditions, compare them to your own classroom today and think about possible changes.

When I have worked through this exercise with teachers, most of them are struck by the power of curiosity to drive learning, engender persistence, and unleash accomplishment. What a great reminder that we can work from kids' own questions backward to the required curriculum, not always the other way around.

How Is Inquiry Different from "Tell and Test" Instruction?

Because inquiry sometimes seems so hard to define, Steph Harvey and I created this chart to highlight the contrasts (2015). Notice that we do not label old-school teaching as "traditional." That's because progressive, student-centered, and inquiry-based learning is just as strong a strand in the American tradition (think John Dewey, Jerome Bruner, Francis Parker) as the skill-and-drill paradigm that has dominated the last three decades.

Obviously, these two paradigms are not new. They represent profoundly different views of childhood, and have been competing for centuries in Americans' school culture. Today, after a long dominance of coverage instruction, inquiry is resurgent because it fits our newer conception of children, learning, and the national interest.

Inquiry Approach Versus Coverage Approach	
Inquiry Approach	*Coverage Approach*
• Student voice and choice	• Teacher selection and direction
• Questions and concepts	• Required topics and isolated facts
• Collaborative work	• Solitary work
• Strategic thinking	• Memorization
• Authentic investigations	• As if/surrogate learning
• Student responsibility	• Student compliance
• Student as knowledge creator	• Student as information receiver
• Interaction and talk	• Quiet and listening
• Teacher as model and coach	• Teacher as expert and presenter
• Cross-disciplinary studies	• One subject at a time
• Multiple resources	• Reliance on a textbook
• Multimodal learning	• Verbal sources only
• Engaging in a discipline	• Hearing about a discipline
• Real purpose and audience	• Extrinsic motivators
• Caring and taking action	• Forgetting and moving to next unit
• Performance and self-assessments	• Filling in bubbles and blanks

What Is Student-Directed Inquiry?

So what is this book's student-directed inquiry approach, and how is it different from other project-based and inquiry-oriented teaching models? Here's a quick sketch of what student-directed inquiry looks like:

- We believe that all students can and must conduct their own research projects at every age level. We recognize that students are being *held back* if they are not supported to conduct their own short investigations from the earliest grades on up.

- We co-plan learning along with students, rather than plan solely as adults and then lead kids through our set plans later. Even when we have a required curriculum, we make room for kids' questions before, during, and after the mandated material.

- Our aim is always to provide the largest possible degree of student voice and choice in every part of the school experience.

- We plan from kids' interests, not just from standards, benchmarks, targets, tests, and the "data desires" of people outside of schools. We build curriculum from kids' wonders and then back-map projects to the relevant standards.

- We respect kids' attraction to relevant, authentic topics they choose for themselves. Inside of mandated units and topics, we seek out the elements that are most interesting to kids, and start with those.

- We start small and build kids' inquiry muscles with lots of practice. Some of our projects are short, lasting five minutes, twenty minutes, an hour, a couple of days. Some topics require far more time than others, so we tailor the schedule to fit the subject. We give kids plenty of chances to build their research skills and strategies through countless smaller, shorter inquiries before we try long inquiry units.

- We actively honor kids' curiosity all day long. We welcome the spontaneous emergence of children's questions. We'll often interrupt an ongoing lesson and make time to honor, capture, and, when possible, investigate a child's wonder.

- Inquiry thrives in a collaborative climate, so we use knowledge from social psychology and group dynamics to create a climate of genuine friendship, support, and collaboration. Partnering and teamwork are an integral part of an inquiry operating system.

- Before asking children to undertake a new activity or strategy, we explicitly model it ourselves.

- We take on new, nonexpert roles in the classroom, such as lead learner, research partner, coach, and facilitator.

- We encourage students to share their inquiry findings with interested audiences. We occasionally will host public events where parents or community members are invited. More often, sharing with the class or with just a few other students provides a suitable and efficient way for kids to go public.

- Our assessment efforts aim to help kids become their own planners, record keepers, goal setters, self-monitors, and reflectors. This includes banking topics for future investigations. As the year moves on, we look to see kids taking on more of this responsibility.

- Individual academic achievement and skill development are not the only important goals of inquiry projects—or of an education. With every investigation, we also want kids to develop their humanity, empathy, and sense of justice. In student-directed inquiries, our kids are constantly looking out to the wider world and asking, "Where do we fit in?" and "What can we do to help?"

Jumping into Inquiry

Something about inquiry makes it seem hard or risky to many of us teachers. Maybe that's partly because we didn't experience much project-based learning when we were kids in school. And in our teacher training, we mostly learned how to teach the regular curriculum the regular way: telling and testing. Once on the job, thanks to No Child Left Behind, many of us were doing scripted lessons and test prep for years, so we never even got a chance to try inquiry approaches. Indeed, we now have many young teachers in the profession who have *never* had a chance to hand over choice and responsibility to kids in the form of an inquiry unit.

And then there is the control issue. Often teachers are proud to say, "I run a tight ship in my classroom." And it's understandable to worry about mutiny among the crew when you suddenly add new or unfamiliar practices. We worry that the kids may come unglued, act out, or misbehave. But inquiry is *not* loose. As you'll see in this book's ten structures, inquiry is a highly planful, orderly, and organized kind of instruction. It's still plenty tight, but it's a different kind of ship.

How Do We Assess Student-Directed Inquiry?

The kinds of inquiry projects in this book don't match up well with traditional assessment tools like worksheets, quizzes, and multiple-choice tests. To begin with, some of the simpler models are so short—taking only five, ten, or twenty minutes—that they scarcely need any formal assessment at all. For example, when you spend five minutes to model your own curiosity, you may be observing kids for their engagement, attention, and perhaps their follow-up comments or questions—but certainly not making a rubric or giving them a grade. But then, as the projects get longer and there's more substance to assess, inquiry learning requires subtle, thoughtful, and varied forms of assessment.

The next pages show some principles that can help us select the most helpful and relevant assessment practices in inquiry-based classrooms.

Best Practice Assessment

» focuses on the knowledge and abilities that are key to Best Practice learning, and on complex whole outcomes and performances of writing, reading, researching, and problem solving, rather than only on isolated subskills

» is usually formative, not summative—and then applies the findings to guide individual students' further learning and to adjust our own teaching

» employs data that is descriptive or narrative, not just scored or numerical

» involves students in developing meaningful responses (for example, asks students to describe what makes a good research report), and calls on them to keep track of and judge their own work

» triangulates, looking at each child from several angles, by drawing on observation, conversation, artifacts, and performances, and by looking at learning over time

» operates as a part of instruction (as in teacher-student conferences), rather than separate from it

» occupies a moderate amount of time, not ruling a teacher's professional life or consuming lots of instruction time

» where possible, abolishes or deemphasizes competitive grading systems

» involves thoughtful collaboration and discussion with other teachers as they visit each other's classrooms and look at student work together

» employs parent-education programs to help community members understand the value of new approaches, and then invites parents to participate in the process

(Zemelman, Daniels, and Hyde 2012, 82)

This chart comes from a book called *Best Practice: Bringing Standards to Life in America's Classrooms*, which I wrote with my partners Steve Zemelman and Arthur Hyde (2012). In this resource, we talk in depth about teaching and assessment K–12, and across the curriculum. The Best Practice Assessment chart here offers some ways we might put these basic principles into action. For every one of these suggestions, there are myriad variations, choices, and styles. Try out options, talk to colleagues, consider digital alternatives, and make it your own.

Tools for the Assessment of Inquiry

Keep your own journal or notebook, including these sections:

1. Your own wonders, questions, and learnings from inside and outside of school. These are topics from your curious life that can be shared with kids.

2. Several pages for each student, where you can jot down what you gradually learn about each individual. This definitely includes personal and out-of-school information in addition to academic insights. As Donald Graves reminded us: until you know ten things about a student, you are not ready to teach that child.

3. Dedicated space to jot teaching notes, save scraps and artifacts, reflect on your lessons, and noodle ideas for future activities.

This kind of log will fill up fast and may need to be replaced periodically.

Set Kids Up to Self-Assess

One of the great strengths of student-directed inquiry is that kids are explicitly asked to take steadily increasing responsibility for their own learning—which also means keeping their own records.

1. Help students create journals, logs, notebooks, or idea books where they can save their own wonderings, learnings about classmates (parallel to your journal section for kid notes), research findings, and personal goal setting. Filling all these functions may require multiple volumes or storage spaces.

2. Help students to set up portfolios (paper, digital, or hybrids) where they can save finished or ongoing work. Periodically hold portfolio maintenance sessions for review, reflection, and updating. Use portfolios as the evidence base in student-led parent conferences.

Document Student Work

1. Hold frequent student conferences about both inquiry procedures and recent findings. Worried about "saying the right thing"? Just try these three prompts: *What are you working on? How is it going? How can I help?* Probe

kids' thinking and decision making; help them set goals for their next investigations. Keep track of any goals they set so you can follow up later.

2. Take pictures and videos of work in progress and of culminating events or artifacts (posters, murals, live reports). Use these images for classroom displays as appropriate, and have kids save copies in their portfolios.

3. Collect artifacts of kids' learning. Save writings, artwork, lists, posters, charts, and sticky notes containing students' thinking or their comments on others' work.

Observe Students at Work

Inquiry teachers can often be seen with a clipboard or tablet in their hands, practicing narrative assessment—writing down in natural, not numerical, language what kids are thinking and doing.

1. Practice kid watching. Look over students' shoulders, interview them, watch from a distance. Write down what you see them saying or doing. For example: While circulating through the room, use sticky notes to jot what you notice about kids' learning, and stick them in the appropriate student's folder when you swing by your desk. Some teachers like to pick five different students each day for more focused observation.

2. Use simple checklists to keep track of where students are in inquiry projects (question posing, searching, sifting sources, discussing with partners, creating a presentation). In longer small-group inquiries, we sometimes have kids create written plans or contracts, and these become a natural tool for assessing progress.

Rubrics and Grading

Many of us work in schools where any extended activity needs to be not just assessed but graded. In those circumstances, the best solution is often a rubric. A scoring rubric, which can be co-created with students, *defines the ingredients of a successful performance on a given activity*. Usually a rubric is constructed by identifying a few critical ingredients of the target activity, and then by defining some levels of performance. Take a look at the general rubric for kids doing mini-inquiries.

Generic inquiry rubric for the mini-inquiry process			
Can the student . . .	Yes	Developing	Not Yet
Pose a question or topic of curiosity?			
Locate information about that topic from different sources?			
Evaluate and choose relevant information?			
Synthesize learning from multiple sources?			
Collaborate on research with others when needed?			
Go public with learning using varied representations?			
Attend to, respond to, and ask questions about classmates' research?			

Here we have seven criteria, each with three possible score levels. If you need to translate this to a grade, you can average and convert students' high, middle, and low scores into your school's grading system. In general, I'd resist the trend toward highly elaborate rubrics with dozens of criteria, standards, targets, levels, cells, descriptors—and hundreds of possible scores. Such hyperdetailed assessments can saddle teachers with long preparation times and unnecessary complexity, with few (or no) additional benefits for students. For some valuable tips and cautions on designing rubrics, see Rick Wormeli's excellent article in the *AMLE Magazine*, "Calling for a 'Timeout' on Rubrics and Grading Scales" (2015).

My extended professional family of teacher-authors has written a good deal more about the assessment of inquiry projects. To look further into these progressive practices, check out *Assessment Live* by Nancy Steineke (2009), *Subjects Matter* by Steve Zemelman and me (2014), and *Amplify* by Katie Muhtaris and Kristin Ziemke (2015).

How to Use This Book

This book offers ten practical ways of starting small, evoking kids' curiosity, and trying out quick investigations. The chapters provide a ladder that leads to more comprehensive and extensive use of inquiry approaches when you are ready.

These structures are

1. Demonstrate your own curiosity

2. Investigate ourselves and our classmates

3. Capture and honor kids' questions

4. Begin the day with soft starts

5. Check your news feed

6. Hang out with an expert

7. Pursue kids' own questions with mini-inquiries

8. Address curricular units with mini-inquiries

9. Lean into a crisis

10. Learn from partners and pioneers.

Each of these approaches has been tested and proven by teachers around the country. Some of these structures you may have heard of before or already dabbled in yourself. Others may have you scratching your head, at least for now. If you are already an inquiry enthusiast, some of these structures may help you expand your repertoire even further.

Each chapter includes three or four lessons from real teachers' classrooms, both primary and intermediate. In these "lesson stories," you'll hear step by step how a teacher tried out the strategy, what kids did and said, what adjustments were needed along the way, and what the outcomes were. As you read, you can be alert for lessons you could adapt to your own classroom—and then give it a try.

The ten structures are arranged roughly in order of increasing complexity and time commitment. The earlier ones take just a few minutes and retain a healthy degree of teacher control. Then, as you move up through the alternatives, they take a bit more time, offer more challenge and complexity, and hand over more responsibility to students. That being said, start anywhere. The main mechanism here is to give kids a chance to show you how trustworthy they can be and how hard they'll work when their curiosity is engaged. Take whatever moments your school days give you and dive in. Even better, find some colleagues to take this journey with you!

Here are some of the features you will consistently find in each chapter.

Point Outs: In the margins, you'll often see quick notes from me, intended to show how you can translate what the teacher on that page is doing right into your own classroom.

Try This: Once in each chapter, I'll encourage you to pause and ponder (alone or with colleagues) how your own thinking works when you are teaching or learning.

Sketchnotes: Each chapter ends with a beautiful and thoughtful sketchnote by my friend and fellow Heinemann author Tanny McGregor. This burgeoning form of graphic note taking is taking the school world by storm, and Tanny is one of its foremost practitioners. As you'll see, her sketchnotes are not linear chapter summaries, but creatively represent one person's real-time journey through a text. As such, they offer plenty to interact with as you sort out your own takeaways from a chapter.

Web Resources: Researching and writing this book provided too much wonderful material to fit between covers. At hein.pub/CuriousClassroom you'll find additional classroom stories, reproducible handouts, links to video clips, and more photos of kids and teachers at work.

On the Web

Come along! Let's start small.

Individual academic achievement and skill development are not the only important goals of inquiry projects—or of an education. With every investigation, we also want kids to develop their humanity, empathy, and sense of justice. In student-directed inquiries, our kids are constantly looking out to the wider world and asking, "Where do we fit in?" and "What can we do to help?"

1

Demonstrate Your Own Curiosity

why

When you regularly mention what you are reading, watching, following, or investigating, you show kids that you are an engaged learner in your "real life."

"Let me show you something I have been wondering and reading and learning about. Here's how I have been investigating my topic. Any questions or comments?"

what

We Might Say to Kids

how

Two to ten minutes; revisit daily, weekly, or throughout the year.

Long It Might Take

When I was a kid in school, seeing your teacher out in public was a mind-blowing shock. Is that her? Right here in the grocery store, buying pickles? *She eats pickles? She eats?*

These blessedly rare encounters did not square well with my assumption that as soon as we students left the classroom, Mrs. Barnard folded up into a small, tidy box until we returned.

As inquiry teachers, we want to present a very different persona to our kids. Instead of impersonating a fold-up robot or a faceless functionary, we want to be real flesh-and-blood (and grown-up appropriate) people. I quoted Donald Graves earlier for famously advising: "You are not ready to teach a child until you know ten things about her life outside of school." As in: Tara has a cat named Chester, she likes butterscotch cookies, her mom is a nurse, she has been to the ocean many times. . . .

Figure 1.1 Jessica Lenz uses a whiteboard to share her personal alligator inquiry with kids.

And maybe kids are not ready to be taught by us until they know ten things about *our* real lives (Figure 1.1).

We have of course all been warned that as teachers we should not be "friends" with our students, and that some distance must be maintained to preserve our authority. We know not to play "truth or dare" with our students. But in our inquiry classrooms, we are less frequently playing the boss/expert role. Instead, we are acting more like a lead learner, a coach, a facilitator, or a willing research colleague. An impersonal, authoritarian stance is less useful in this kind of relationship; indeed, it calls for something like the opposite. Social psychology research has long shown that true authority comes not from your job title or your ability to reward or punish, but from *friendship* and *perceived expertise* (Schmuck and Schmuck 2000).

When I am doing demonstration lessons around the country, here's one way I share my own curious life with students I've just met. Maybe it would work for you. I project a two-column chart of my wonderings—a format I learned from my colleague James Beane (2006). On one side, I list my current *self* questions—my personal, local concerns. (I sometimes call these my "me, me, me" wonders.) On the other side are my *world* questions, wider topics that many other people also wonder about. Figure 1.2 shows a recent version.

Don't get me started on the asteroid thing. But I'll just say, we have to get working on this *right now*, people.

Next, I'll invite kids to make their own self/world question lists. This takes some time and patience; you quickly find that very few of us, kids or grown-ups, can instantly access all the questions we are carrying around in our heads. But they're in there (see the upcoming "Try This" feature). When I did this lesson with kids at the Tesuque Owingeh Pueblo School, Jessica Gonzalez' second and third graders spent a full ten minutes talking over and gradually jotting down some ideas. In the end, these students came up with dozens of great inquiry topics, many reflective of their life on a rural New Mexico reservation.

Self	World
Why is dry cleaning so expensive?	What international relief agencies are most trustworthy?
How long will my knees last if I keep hiking in the mountains?	Will the drought in the southwest USA continue?
Are paper plates an ecological disaster—really?	How can we enlist more people of color into the teaching profession?
What "super foods" should I be eating?	Why and how is the circus *finally* phasing out elephant acts?
How long will my 2003 Highlander last?	How could we defend the planet from an asteroid impact?
What was that masked animal at my window last week?	What happens if Los Alamos Lab leaks, explodes, or gets attacked?

Figure 1.2 Smokey's self and world questions

Try This

Having a hard time surfacing your own inquiry questions? Feeling short on curiosity? You're not. Just take a few minutes and think through this list of prompts that I often show to kids or teachers. Jot down any questions that get triggered as you think. I guarantee you'll recover at least three questions from the back burner of your brain. (This activity is also great for a workshop or faculty meeting.)

An "idle" question
A book or author you are reading
A place you have always wanted to visit
A topic you are wondering about
An item you saw in the news
A person who has puzzled you recently
The last thing you googled
If I had a bucket list, _____ would be on it
An issue you're investigating to solve a problem
A purchase or investment you're pondering
A student question that stuck in your mind
A topic from your childhood
Whatever happened to . . .
Something you have always wanted to explore

See, you are just brimming with inquiry topics. Pick one that might interest your students, open up your head (metaphorically), and show it to them.

We can share aspects of our own lives any old time, just to deepen our acquaintance with kids. But our own experiences can also enliven curricular units. As a fourth-grade teacher in Wisconsin, Daniel Argyres is required to teach a unit on immigration. One of the centers he creates for kids is about Ellis Island, and among the artifacts on display are the authentic immigration papers and photos of his grandfather, Emmanuel Leonidas Argyriades (shortened to Argyres) as he emigrated from Greece to America through Ellis Island on May 29, 1927. (Amazingly enough, Daniel also has the records for his *great-grandfather*, John Konstantakopoulos, shortened to John Kondos, who also emigrated to America through Ellis Island on January 8, 1904.) All these documents reveal powerful details of the journey through the strangeness and the bureaucracy of American immigration in the 1900s. Daniel is a scholar of his ancestors, his family, and the Greek culture. Kids who study immigration with him are getting it up close and personal, not from the watered-down textbook "coverage."

Coming up, you'll see how teachers from all corners of America let students in on their curious lives, sharing their reading habits, their personal challenges, their risk taking, and even how they learn along with fellow teachers.

SHARE YOUR OUT-OF-SCHOOL LIFE
My terrible feet

Megan Dixon, second-grade teacher at Glenwood School

To build positive relationships with students and promote classroom community, Megan Dixon tries to learn one new thing about each of her students every week (meaning she must discover something new about five or six kids a day). Like Aerianna loves everything about San Francisco. Lukas is fascinated with cars and engines. Isaac's favorite band is the Decemberists. And Alana is absolutely terrified of chickens.

For her part, Megan tries to share something about herself from the first day of school to the very last. Just think: 180 pieces of Megan's identity that she steadily offers up to connect more and more deeply with kids. Sometimes, this modeling just entails talking about a book she's currently reading, a new strategy she learned from a teacher magazine, or the antics of her own rambunctious and stubborn six-year-old, who will put on a dress or skirt only when riding her scooter or bike, but definitely not on holidays or special occasions. While much of

Megan's personal sharing takes place during class meetings, at other times it comes up naturally in response to—or as part of—a lesson, investigation, or read-aloud.

At one particular class meeting, Megan shared a personal breakthrough. As she explains: "I have always been an athlete. I pounded the pavement in high school basketball and in high school and college tennis. I have always been very active, but my joints got so bad that I had to give up running, one of my favorite pastimes. My narrow, high-arched feet were causing numerous knee and hip problems, several months of physical therapy, new shoes and foot inserts, and finally a new exercise routine. This was a huge loss to me. So my news today, something I was eager to share with my class, was that I was finally feeling healthy enough to start running again after years."

Now it made sense to the kids why Mrs. Dixon *never* wore fancy shoes, was sometimes spotted walking around barefoot, and often complained about her terrible feet. Megan told the kids how nervous and excited she was to begin running again, after two years. She showed kids a website she had used to find the best shoes for her troubled tootsies. Then she shared an article about setting up a running regimen.

As Megan described these resources she'd accessed, the students were genuinely interested, encouraging, and supportive of her efforts. Seizing the moment, Megan brought out a calendar and in front of the students set a goal to run at least three times a week and work up to a ten-minute pace for four miles. Then, she hung up the calendar in a spot where all students could see it and check up on her every day.

The chart held her accountable to herself—and the kids. It was common to hear students ask, "Hey, Mrs. Dixon, did you run this morning?" or "Are you on track to meet your goal?" and to gently chide her if she missed a day. Enrique, one of the first students to arrive each day, checked in on a daily basis. Frequently, he would look at the calendar to make sure that his teacher had updated the morning's mileage. Knowing she had a difficult time running in the evening after being on her feet all day, he would say, "Mrs. Dixon, you know if you don't run in the morning, you won't do it!"

Every day she ran, Megan wrote the time and distance on the calendar, coming closer and closer to meeting her goal. One day in the middle of her running project, she labeled a place next to her calendar with the heading "What's *your* goal?"

Without prompting, students began placing sticky notes with their own goals (see Figure 1.3). Some were out-of-school activities, like Megan's:

- Help mom more with the baby

- Play outside one hour each day

- Get better at swimming by doing the length of the pool nonstop

- Walk four miles with my mom

Figure 1.3 Nevy's goal was to help her mother with the baby for one hundred days.

Others were academic; the kids' excitement spread to any type of goal:

- I will read 30 minutes at night.

- I will finish the Magic Tree House series.

- I won't be a "log" during book club.

Not surprisingly, students asked if they could have their own blank calendars so that they could begin tracking their progress toward their goals.

These kid goals then became another topic at daily meetings and a venue to encourage and support each other. Megan concludes the story: "It was not uncommon for students to write each other encouraging notes and leave them for each other in their mailboxes. The kids and I celebrated each and every goal met. When I finally hit my running target, a student wrote a note saying, 'We are all

Figure 1.4 Megan's workout calendar at the end of her training

proud of you for working so hard to reach your goal' and had the whole class sign it. Noel gave us daily updates on her walking goal with her mom. We gave her a rousing round of applause when she reached ten thousand steps! What started as my own quick share turned into a model of living a curious life, goal setting, supporting each other to achieve goals, and problem solving. And I'm still running, carefully." (See Megan's completed workout calendar in Figure 1.4.)

TALK ABOUT YOUR READING

What are you reading, Mrs. McG?

Tanny McGregor, teaching in a third-grade class in Withamsville-Tobasco School

Tanny McGregor, who has taught for twenty-eight years, now works as a classroom consultant and coach for her Ohio district. When I asked Tanny to tell how she shares her reading life with kids, she immediately thought of this lesson:

> It is always a pleasure to have Rachel Ryba on my coaching schedule. She's always up for new ideas, and her students mirror their teacher's love for learning. One morning in May, I climbed the steps to Rachel's classroom, typical lesson materials in hand: some photographs, a piece of text to explore, a few sheets of chart paper, colored markers. I had a plan. And the plan was to stick with the plan.
>
> I had barely crossed the classroom threshold when a grinning boy greeted me, offering to help me carry my things over to the meeting area. A few other kids soon joined us on the rug. They were continuing the conversation that had been going on while they waited for me to arrive, talking

about books they'd read lately and what they planned to read over the summer break.

As if not wanting me to feel left out, that same helpful boy looked up at me and asked, "So what are you reading, Mrs. McG?" That question always makes me smile. I answered quickly. After all, I had a lesson to teach. "I'm reading historical fiction, the story of a little girl who hunted fossils." I set up my teaching area, easel to my right, markers at the ready. "Her name was Mary Anning."

I called the other students over to the large group area, and proceeded with the minilesson. I honestly don't remember what the skill or strategy focus was that day. What I do remember is that as soon as the lesson ended, the same small group of kids surrounded me as I packed up. "Did she find any fossils?" "How old was she?" "Where did she live?" I answered their questions, promising to bring my copy of *Remarkable Creatures* when I visited next.

Later that day I began thinking about what had happened. Not so much a reflection about the lesson, but about what happened *before* and *after* the lesson. These kids were curious. They were intensely interested in what I was reading. They were asking questions. They were talking about books. Wasn't this exactly what we always say we want kids to be and do? These thoughts faded as I started planning for my next visit to Rachel's class.

But, luckily, a copy of *Remarkable Creatures* by Tracy Chevalier was tucked into my backpack as I returned the next day. As soon as the lesson was over, I said, "Hey, if anyone is interested in hearing about the book I'm reading, stay on the carpet a little while longer." Everyone stayed. I shared how Mary Anning, a ten-year old girl and budding paleontologist in Lyme Regis, England, collected "curiosities" (later known as fossils) to sell. She had to make money for her family since her father had died. Over time well-known scientists from London heard about Mary's expertise uncovering and identifying these bones. When she was twelve she discovered the remains of an Ichthyosaur. "These things really happened!" I told the students. "I am so curious about Mary now, I've been doing my own research. So many facts are woven into this story." I held the book in my hands, showing everyone how I still had quite a bit to read. Questions and connections came pouring forth. No surprise, since passion is contagious. "Was she the first girl paleontologist?" "She was just a little older than we are." "Did she become famous?" "Is she ever mentioned in science books?" "Maybe it was hard for her to become a scientist back then since she was a girl."

Finally I began to awaken from my lesson plan stupor. C'mon, Mc-Gregor! What are you waiting for?

POINT OUT

Even when we are teaching a required curricular lesson, we should always keep our ears open for great kids' questions that we can capture and come back to later, when we have time.

These kids are genuinely interested in learning about a child from long ago who changed the scientific history. They are using strategic thinking, and they are primed and ready to investigate. Get out of the way and let it happen!

The next class was different. I brought in several picture books and articles about Mary Anning's life and discoveries. We read about, talked through, and searched for answers to our questions. We even stumbled upon a song by the band Artichoke that detailed Mary's story, reading the lyrics closely while the music pulled us in. Everyone so engaged. Everyone so curious.

I later learned that these students had recently been studying about fossils in science class. Did their curiosity stem from new content knowledge? Perhaps. I'd like to think so. But maybe the reason isn't so important. What matters is that we were reading and talking together, collecting curiosities like Mary Anning did more than two hundred years ago.

A whole-class inquiry started with one student's question: So what are you reading, Mrs. McG?

SHOW HOW YOU TAKE A RISK
Carolynn, are you going to cry?

Carolynn Klein Hageman, first-grade teacher at Duke School

First-grade teacher Carolynn Klein got up early one school day and noticed a one-quart Pyrex measuring cup left out on her kitchen counter. She reached up to put the glass vessel back where it belonged, on a high cabinet shelf. Later on, Carolynn reflected that she might not have been quite awake enough for such a risky operation. But in the moment, the measuring cup fell right back off the shelf and hit her smack on the forehead. The cup didn't break, a testament to its sturdy design, but it did put a pretty nasty cut in Carolynn's right eyebrow as it bounced off her face.

A certified tough cookie, Carolynn put the cup away securely, stanched the blood flow with paper towels, and then drove off to do her job at school. The first colleague to spot her in the teachers' work room said, "Whoa, that's quite a wound you've got there," and insisted on getting her a butterfly bandage.

Right about then, a student's dad, dressed for his workout at the local gym, walked through to drop his daughter off for school. Since Dr. Ryan Lamb was an emergency room physician at the local hospital, Carolynn asked him what he thought of her wound. "That definitely needs stitches," he advised.

Carolynn shook her head, concluding, "OK, thanks for that info. I guess I'll get someone to cover my class while I go and get this sewn up."

"Don't do that," he said. "I'm off today—let me go grab my bag and I will come back and stitch you up."

"You mean here?"

"Sure, just let me run back home and get my doctor bag and I'll see you in ten minutes."

"Wow, OK, great," Carolynn thought as the doctor drove off. Now she wondered where and how this procedure would take place, when it suddenly occurred to her: this was the mother of all teachable moments, especially since her class was in the middle of a health unit. Talk about sharing your curious life with kids! Carolynn could get her stitches right in front of her six-year-old students.

She considered the downsides: some kids might be frightened by this "too real" spectacle, so there had to be an easy way for the queasy to opt out. On the plus side, many kids had already bragged about their own accidents, cuts, and stitch-ups.

You don't need to share something *this* personal just to prove to your kids that you're "real"! Always select a level of self-disclosure that's comfortable for you and the children.

POINT OUT

And a recent expert visitor had been a local surgeon who showed kids how to sew up a wound, and even had them practice with needles and thread on torn burlap. Carolynn, who always tells kids her personal motto is "go with the flow," decided to go for it. Just to be on the safe side, she checked with the school's curriculum director, who grabbed a camera by way of assent.

Dr. Lamb returned with his bag. As the father of a classmate in this small school community, he needed little introduction. Before Carolynn lay down on the rug (normally used for gentle read-alouds and class meetings), she and the doctor told the kids exactly what was going to happen. They explained that anyone who didn't want to watch could sit in the very back of the room and continue their independent reading. Three boys immediately retired (they crept back when the action started). Most of the other kids pulled in close for a better view.

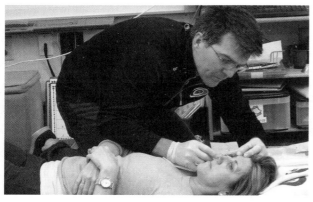

Figure 1.5 Carolynn receives stitches on the classroom floor as kids ask questions.

Soon Carolynn was comfortably laid out on the rug in her classroom, swaddled with comfy blankets and pillows. (See the patient in Figure 1.5.) The doctor knelt at her side, his black bag standing open. He pulled out the instruments he would need and showed each one to the class, explaining how he was going to use it.

One of the kids blurted out: "Carolynn, are you going to cry?" (Kids use teachers' first names at Duke School.)

"Well, I *could*," she answered. "But I don't think I will. I've had stitches before and I know it only feels like a tiny pinch. I also know that Dr. Lamb has lots of experience giving people stitches."

The children began peppering him with questions too:

- What's the most stitches you have had to give someone?

- What is the most common reason people get stitches?

- How many people do you stitch in a day?

- What part of the body gets the most stitches?

- How much time do you have after an accident to get the stitches done?

- How do you know a cut needs stitches and not just a bandage?

- What is the worst reason someone has had to get stitches?

The doctor patiently answered all of their spontaneous questions as he got ready. He inserted his syringe into a bottle of lidocaine, explaining every step as he made several small injections. Next, he showed how he threads the curved needle. He proceeded with the stitches—one, two, three. He talked about how he ties the thread and how Carolyn should care for her stitches after he's done. Carolynn assured the kids that she was feeling no pain, just a little pulling sensation.

In the literacy world, when an adult models and vocalizes her thinking during a complex activity, we call it a "think-aloud." Usually, we practice this strategy while reading a book or writing a story, but the procedure turns out to work just as well for first aid. The world's first "stitch-aloud." Who knew?

DEMONSTRATE INQUIRY AS A FACULTY TEAM
There's a virus inside us

Amber Ankrom, Annie Gentithes, Becca Woolridge, Claudia Michelman, Elaine Cameron, Meghan Morris, Michelle Reich, K–8 Faculty at Duke School, Durham, North Carolina

We teachers don't just have to model our *individual* curiosity for students. In this example, seven faculty members from Duke School conducted an inquiry and took their learning public with the whole school community.

In early December last year, many of our students and teachers were out of school with a miserable flu. Most of us, children and adults, had dutifully gotten our flu shots, but we were all getting sick anyway. Our attendance was decimated. As a faculty, we were concerned and wanted to know more about the problem we were noticing. Our (uber-fantastic) librarian Elaine rallied faculty members to use this as an opportunity to model our own curiosity and collaboration.

Driven by the initial question we had been pondering over the preceding weeks—why are so many of us getting sick?—we each investigated an aspect of the flu epidemic that was of personal interest to us. Teachers investigated a range of topics, such as treatments, symptoms, strains, and vaccines, learning from print and Internet resources as well as by interviewing experts within the community.

POINT OUT

These teachers are inventing something rarely seen in our schools—a teacher team inquiry with a product displayed for students. What a fantastic way to model the collaborative, small-group investigations that are the basic formation for so many student inquiries.

Michelle called her pediatrician and asked her if this year's flu shot would afford partial protection, even if the strain in the vaccine is incorrect. Becca studied the CDC website and found out the difference between the shot and the nasal spray. Elaine researched the different flu strains and how researchers pick which ones to include in the vaccine each year.

Each teacher not only investigated a different question, but also represented his or her findings in a unique way that made sense. We created a large display right in the campus library, so passing students from all grade levels could stop and have a look. There were graphs, drawings, statistics, and narrative representations. [See Figures 1.6 and 1.7.] We reprinted some key articles we had read, highlighting in yellow the passages that helped us answer our big research questions. Annie drew a diagram to help her visualize the respiratory system. Elaine surveyed every class to compile statistics on absences and displayed the information in a graph.

We wanted our postings to be just as diverse as the inquiry work we aim to do with students all year long. Talk about going viral! Our display demonstrated the power of collective curiosity, the value of wondering, and the importance of bringing our community together. To top it off, it was fun!

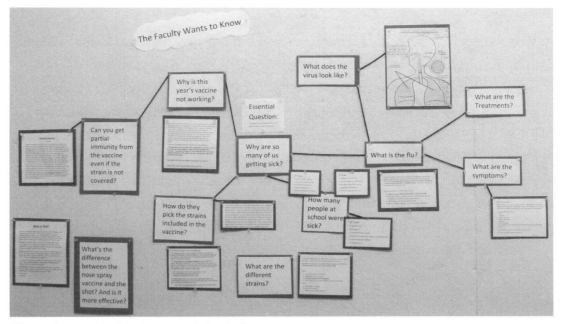

Figure 1.6 Faculty learnings chart about viruses

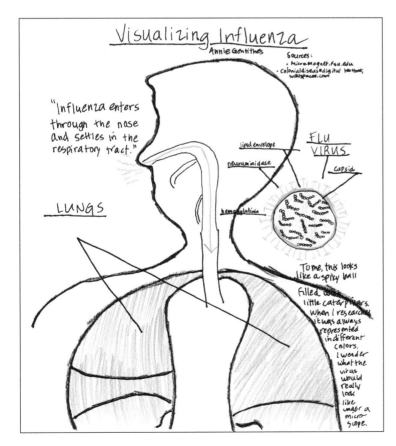

Figure 1.7 Visualizing influenza and how it infects us

We teachers have been shy to reveal much about our personal lives to our students (and in some categories, we are probably wise to do so). And maybe we are not quite ready to lie down and receive medical treatment on the floor of our classrooms. But the teachers at Duke, Glenwood, and Withamsville-Tobasco schools found it fun and satisfying to model their own thinking for kids. I think they felt the magnetic attraction of "getting real," of occasionally dropping the teacher/expert persona, and of just being a learner on a team with others. Today's kids, no matter what kind of community they come from, urgently need to see as many thoughtful, curious, resourceful, and critical adults as they can. Even if some of those people have terrible feet.

2

Investigate Ourselves and Our Classmates

why

The baseline curiosity questions in any classroom or community are *Who am I?* and *Who are we?* Deepening our self-knowledge and broadening our acquaintances help grow a supportive climate where curiosity and risk taking are always welcome.

"There are so many interesting people in here! What can we share about ourselves? What questions do we have about each other? The better we get to know everyone in the room, the better we can work together and have fun exploring new ideas."

what
We Might Say to Kids

how
Long It Might Take

Five to ten minutes each session; repeat five to ten times over the early weeks of school.

Sometimes, when I am describing a particular inquiry project, a teacher will blurt out: "My kids could never do that!" Usually this means that her students seem too fractious, too discordant, too ill behaved to operate in a decentralized, collaborative situation. Read: the kids don't get along well enough to be trusted with this sort of work. Probably they have never been in a highly interactive classroom in their previous school lives, either. I have taught in and visited such classrooms. This concern is real.

Sometimes we teachers feel that the trustworthiness of our students is just the luck of the draw, and dream that "maybe next year I'll get a class that can do inquiry." But supportive classrooms are not just mysteriously dealt out; they can be *made* from the raw materials that are delivered to us each fall. We can take affirmative steps from the start of the year to dramatically raise the odds of growing a collaborative group of students who can take responsibility for challenging and cooperative inquiries all year long.

So what's the formula for creating a cohesive class? From day one, we work explicitly on both *identity* and *acquaintance*. Identity work is vital since, as psychologists Thomas Allen and Jeffrey Sherman have shown, "When people feel bad about themselves, they are more likely to show bias against people who are different" (2011). Translated to the classroom, this reminds us that kids need a strong positive identity in order to develop empathy toward others, especially classmates who seem different or unknown. So we begin with a repertoire of quick interactions that help kids gain insight into their own traits, interests, character, experiences, beliefs—and then share them with others in a controlled and comfortable way.

What assumptions do we build from? Here's one: people like people they know. Obvious, right? But think about this. Much discord in the world (and in schools) comes from our ignorance of one another. People don't know someone, so they assume the worst and act accordingly. Conversely, the more you get to know someone, the harder it gets to hate, belittle, or bully them. Social psychology teaches us that most times, acquaintance leads to friendliness, which leads to supportive behavior. The stakes are high: genuine inquiry work requires kids to rely on every classmate as a potential partner, coinvestigator, or audience for the topic they are pursuing (Daniels and Steineke 2014).

If you think about it, the process of "getting to know" someone proceeds by gradual and mutual self-disclosure. With a new district colleague, we might have a conversation like this:

What grade do you teach?

Third, over at Washington.

Me too, third at Hamilton.

Small world.

Did you grow up around here?

On a farm in the county. Dairy.

Does your family still own it?

Yes, my dad works it with my brother.

I grew up in town here; my family had the hardware store.

The Ace?

Yup. So did you go to Northern, then?

No, I went away to State. Always wanted to be a teacher.

Hah, me too. I set up a pretend classroom in my basement and made the other kids sit there while I taught them.

You have a family?

My husband, Tim. He's an electrical contractor.

Gary is a drywall guy—I wonder if they've worked together.

And I have two kids. They are two and five. Here's a picture.

Adorable! One of each, lucky you. My daughter just got married. I have some pictures of the wedding.

Let's see them . . .

Try This

If you're doing this work on your own, think of a person in your life you'd like to know better. This could be an existing acquaintance, neighbor, relative, student, or, what the heck, your old college roomie whom you could call on the phone.

If you are reading this book as part of a teacher study group, PLC, or college class, potential better friends are sitting right in front of you! Set aside some time and ask everyone to seek out someone they don't already know well or work with often. Change your regular seats if needed! Then pairs select one of the topics below and have a ten-minute conversation, taking turns and asking each other follow-up questions. This should be a natural back-and-forth chat, not sequential soliloquies. You can use a note-taking strategy if you want to remember information, but don't let it impede the flow.

What to talk about:

- Talk about the *neighborhoods* where you grew up.
- Talk about some *accidents* that have affected your life
- Share some favorite *family stories*

In reality, this process we call "getting acquainted" simply means exchanging bits of our identity with another person, back and forth, over time, in a controlled way. As we get to know more and more about each other, we almost always feel increasingly positive and friendly toward the other person. Indeed, we often begin calling them a *friend*.

In this chapter, you'll encounter a whole batch of brief but practical lessons teachers have devised to build identity, friendliness, and support in their classrooms. I was lucky enough to see these contributors in their schools in Chicago, California, Wisconsin, New York, and New Mexico. Such different cultures, but such similar classroom climates when the identity and empathy work has been done.

To summarize all this: if you want a curious, collaborative, inquiry-ready classroom, then you are in the friendship-creating business. Start early and enjoy it!

GET TO KNOW OUR IDENTITIES

How do I see myself?

Beth Kaminski, first-grade teacher; **Megan Dixon**, second-grade teacher; and **Deb Zaffiro**, instructional coach at Glenwood School
Kristin Ziemke, first-grade teacher at Big Shoulders Foundation
Sara Ahmed, sixth-grade teacher at The Bishop's School

Each of these closely related variations shows a different way of inviting kids to map, draw, or otherwise represent their own identities. Rather than using out-loud discussions to surface these potentially tender topics, we offer quiet think time with a graphic model that allows kids a safe and thoughtful path toward sharing with others.

Identity Maps

At Glenwood School, kids in the primary grades create identity maps to share their lives, get to know their classmates, and generate ideas for later research and writing. Since most of these kids learn the concept of webbing at ages four and five in the school's kindergartens, children are ready and eager to try out this new form of mapping when they hit first grade.

The basic concept is simple: students put their name (or their self-portrait) in the center of a big sheet of drawing/poster paper and then branch off, listing things they care about—family, favorites, important memories—and topics on which they might be experts. Of course, kids do this only after their teacher demonstrates it first, using a list of possible identity topics (see Sara Ahmed's list on the next page). Through this modeling process, students learn fascinating personal information about their teacher and become extra excited to begin their own webs.

Identity

Personality	Favorite foods
Physical Features	Age
Opinions, beliefs	Gender
Perspective	How you treat others
Family	Financial status
Culture	Reactions
Ethnicity	Sportsmanship
Language	Lifestyle
Religion	Job
Environment & Community	Traditions
Nationality	Celebrations

Figure 2.1 is a recent identity web of my own that I started in front of a class to show kids the idea, and then gradually completed as children worked on their own webs along with me.

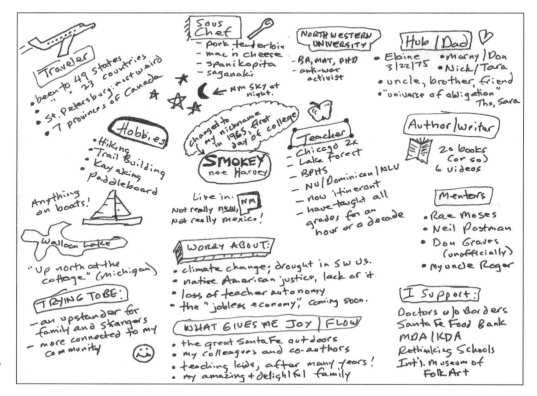

Figure 2.1

A recent identity web for Smokey

If my example looks quite detailed and illustrated, this is something that kids have taught me. Sure, they can sketch out something in a minute or two. But given a little extra time, they will invest extraordinary effort and artistic care in making these maps of themselves. In fact, we often see a lull after a couple minutes of web work time—followed by a second surge of detail, expansion, and illustration. As students construct their webs, conversations often break out in table groups and kids begin to learn about each other even before the web is complete.

Here are a couple of sample webs from Glenwood School last year, collected for us by instructional coach Deb Zaffiro.

In Beth's class, kids made their webs with very limited time, but most elaborated fully. As you can see in Figure 2.2, David has a twin brother, is a lover of facts (I hope he runs for office someday), and is a rescuer of endangered animals. Quite a resume for a six-year-old—and so much to talk about with your friends.

In Megan's room, her second-grade mapping veterans wanted to experiment with the format. Mason (see Figure 2.3) listed *places* he likes on the left (Disney World, Home, Blue Harbor, and his cousin's house) and *things* he likes on the right (math, science, reading, writing, family). Hey, Mason, #JoinMyClassNextYear!

Kelsey obviously leaves no doubt about who rocks! Perhaps borrowing Mason's left/right layout, she has carefully arranged the things she loves (dogs, my friends, and ramen soup) and hates (spiders, horror movies, and when I'm too short to go on an amusement park ride) on opposite sides of her web (Figure 2.4).

We usually have kids create identity webs early in the year, when we are intentionally working on positive self-identity and

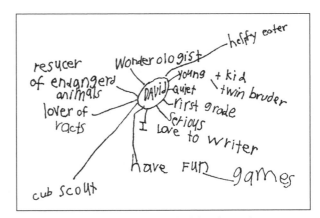

Figure 2.2 First grader David's identity web

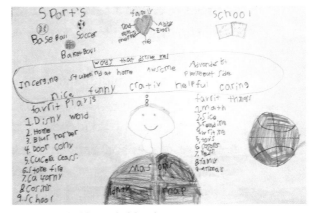

Figure 2.3 Mason's identity map

Figure 2.4
Kelsey's identity map

group collaboration. The next step is for students to share their webs with others, in a context that feels safe and comfortable. This might mean with one partner, a table group, or ideally the whole class. We like to hang the maps at well-spaced intervals around the room, and then have kids visit several classmates' charts. They bring along sticky notes and leave behind comments about connections ("I love dogs too!") or questions ("What amusement park did you go to?"). We leave them hanging for days and make time for kids to "meet at our webs" and talk.

Partner Venns

First-grade teacher Kristin Ziemke has pairs of kids use these familiar overlapping circles to create a partner web. She suggests you "go big" and do this on poster or chart paper, so kids can work side by side on the floor, at a big table, or on pushed-together desks. And when you or the kids draw the circles, be sure to make plenty of room in the middle space for the commonalities.

Kids begin working quietly, each on their side of the diagram, filling in attributes of their own identity. (If they need topic suggestions, you can co-create one fresh or adapt the Identity chart of suggested categories on page 26.) Next, have kids study each other's side of the diagram, looking for things they have in common (e.g., we both like to read, both have a big brother, both bring lunch to

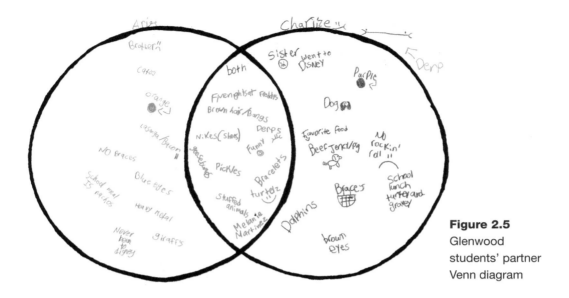

Figure 2.5
Glenwood students' partner Venn diagram

school, both speak Spanish). As they find these, they take turns copying them down in the center section.

Now invite kids to talk about other possible overlaps that might not be listed on both sides—or even on one side. As they keep talking, kids will notice other similarities (we both have brown eyes, we both have on Nike shirts, we play together at lunch).

To share similarities and differences across the whole classroom, hang up the posters at well-spaced intervals and have a gallery walk where kids can examine other peoples' diagrams. Visitors can bring a clipboard on which to create a running list of all the things that students in the class have in common—and bring those lists to a later meeting on the rug.

There are so many delicious variations of these "me" charts. Kids can map:

- What people say about me
- Questions I have about my identity
- What I hope my identity will be in the future
- Identities of book characters and historical figures

POINT OUT

Personal Pie Charts

For kids who are studying fractions or percentages, this identity activity is a natural. But kindergartners and sixth graders are also happy to take a whack at it!

For extra fun, start by projecting an image of a yummy pie and talk about how we cut it up into sections to eat. Then show kids an example of a pie chart—a cool kind of drawing we can use to show how various things get divided up.

Now have kids think about a typical day in their lives and brainstorm a list of the different ways they usually divide their time. You can start this as a whole-class brainstorm, but should switch to individual writing so kids can add in their own unique activities. Common entries I've seen:

- Sleeping
- Getting dressed
- Eating meals
- Arguing with my sister
- Talking to parents
- Riding the bus
- Doing homework
- Being in class
- Playing sports
- Hanging out with friends
- Dreaming
- Playing video games
- Reading
- Watching TV
- Using my phone/ computer

Figure 2.6 My 24, by Sydney

Have kids estimate the hours or minutes they spend on each item on their list, jotting the numbers down beside each activity. Little ones can go straight to the next step and make their pie charts (see Figure 2.6). Older kids can grab calculators or apps to convert their minute totals to more precise percentages. Give kids large sheets of blank paper and colored markers, and let them create their pie charts. Allow ample work time. Share the charts in pairs or hang them throughout the room and have a gallery walk during which students visit several classmates' charts, looking for similarities and differences. They can make notes as they walk around, jotting down questions to ask later when the group reconvenes. Like all the other getting-to-know-each-other inquiries in this chapter, the pie charts helps kids explore their own and others' identities as we build toward a high-morale team that's ready to work together as friends.

EXPLORE OUR DIFFERENCES AS ASSETS

Step in, step out

Ashley Ohmstede, fifth-grade teacher at Eason Elementary School

Fifth-grade teacher Ashley Ohmstede (and the rest of her grade-level team) begins the year with short personal inquiries that get kids better and better acquainted. One of Ashley's favorite structures for this is "Step In, Step Out" (sometimes also called "Cross the Line"). This quick stand-up activity is a great way for kids to explore the variety of identities, personalities, and differences that exist within any classroom. The steps are simple, but the work can get deep and personal.

First, Ashley has kids move back to the edges of the room (or stand behind a line on the floor).

Next, Ashley or a student volunteer calls out an interest/hobby/belief and students step into the middle on any items they agree with. As soon as they have "voted" and finished any discussion, everyone steps back and waits for the next prompt. Ashley usually starts by moving at a quick pace through noncontroversial, getting-acquainted topics and later moves on to mild opinion questions.

Low-Risk Examples

I like pizza.

I have a sister.

I have a brother.

I am an only child.

I am left-handed.

I have brown eyes.

I moved here recently.

I like to dance.

I have traveled to another state.

My best subject is math.

I enjoy sports.

I prefer music over sports.

I think art is one of the best specials at our school.

I think kids should have more than one recess per day.

I don't mind having homework once in a while.

When the class moves to opinion questions, it's natural to ask one or two kids who "stepped over the line" to explain their reasoning.

On any item, Ashley or kids can pause the stepping and ask: What are we noticing? What just happened? What can we say about our class? Ashley explains: "Step In, Step Out works best when there is tons of discussion. Students are invited to be honest in their thoughts, but it's not supposed to spark a right-wrong debate. We just aim for kids to say what they think and feel in a safe structure. Through getting to know one another in this way, students can't help but to want to ask more questions of each other. By exploring differences, they find more of what they have in common, too."

After kids engage with these initial low-risk identity topics, we can progressively introduce more challenging, personal, self-disclosing topics, such as:

Boys are better in math than girls. (gender)

A college education is important. (education)

I celebrate Ramadan. (religion)

People should learn English if they move to America. (language)

It's fine for a family to have two moms or two dads. (family)

There are more opportunities in life when you live in a big city. (location)

Topics like these need to be taken one at a time, and require plenty of respectful discussion. Carefully moderated, these courageous conversations allow kids to demystify difference, and even to see differences as assets. These experiences set us up to talk about creating a safe, friendly, and supportive classroom culture that can support our investigations of intense and serious topics throughout the year. Teachers keep track of body language and are alert to any rising tensions as the prompts come up; they feel free to skip or cancel a topic that, for the moment, looks too provocative.

POINT OUT

When you first try this getting-acquainted activity, make a list of topics that are suitable for your kids and community. The trick is to evoke some real depth of sharing without triggering any discomfort.

With older kids, you can also flip these yes-no identity questions into a "four corners" or "where do you stand" activity. Taking a debatable topic like "kids should not have cell phones in elementary school classrooms," you invite students to stand in sections of the room you have prelabeled *strongly agree*, *agree*, *disagree*, and *strongly disagree*. When students arrive at the spot aligned with their opinion (standing with other kids who agree with them), they chat briefly about their beliefs for a few minutes. Then, you disperse them into "opposing" groups with *different* beliefs, where they share and hear others' opinions.

SHARE OUR LANGUAGES

How's your saya?

Elaine Daniels, professor at Santa Fe Community College

At the start of Elaine Daniels' writing class in Santa Fe, it quickly emerged that students spoke nine different languages: English, Spanish, Guatemalan Spanish, German, Portuguese, French, Korean, Ukrainian, and Tewa, a local Pueblo Indian language (or ten, if you counted one student's Kentucky-rooted dialect he called "Backwoods-ese"). As a way of building community around these differences and assets, Elaine suggested the class have a language fair, a session where each student would teach the class something about his or her first, or home, language.

POINT OUT

As you meet your students early in the year, find out about their home languages. If you find a diversity of tongues, this lesson can build friendship and some beginning knowledge of other cultures.

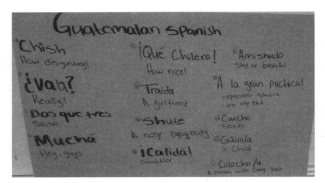

Figure 2.7 Poster made by students sharing their home language with the class

Elaine set a date for the language festival a few days ahead, giving students some time to prepare a quick lesson, get help from families, and make a poster to support their presentation (see an example in Figure 2.7). The basic requirement was to bring five words and a few interesting phrases. Monolingual English speakers were invited to study up on another language they were curious about and bring some words and phrases to share.

The day of the event was one of the most energetic of the year. Among the word items savored by the class were:

Guatemalan:	*chich!*	how disgusting!
Italian:	*chittoro*	guitar
Portuguese	*pao de queijo*	a cheesy bread
French:	*chuchoter*	whisper
Korean:	*sil-le-hahm-ni-da*	excuse me!
German:	*weihnachtsbaum*	Christmas tree
Backwoods-ese:	*crowger*	slob, messy person
Tewa:	*saya*	grandma

One of the most precious outcomes of the language fair came when the two Native American students, normally very private about tribal life, shared moving personal details of their struggles learning the endangered language of their tribe. As you noticed from the heading, this lesson happened in a community college class taught by a close relative of mine. But it fits in this book because it can so easily be adapted to any grade level in today's increasingly multilingual classrooms.

Our language lies at the heart of our identities; it is the main tool we use to explore and engage in the world. Sometimes these days, language differences can become a point of conflict or misunderstanding; instead of letting that happen, we can dive right into it and savor the differences. And as our kids build deeper acquaintance with each other, and develop more and more supportive relationships, we gain the strength to tackle the team efforts of inquiry learning.

DEVELOP A MORNING GREETING RITUAL

Peace, love, and understanding, inc.

Faith Shellabarger, **Katie Block**, **Abby Schmitz**, and **Ashley Ohmstede**, fifth-grade teachers at Eason Elementary School

The fifth-grade team at Eason Elementary was bummed. They had noticed that students were constantly ignoring morning work and rarely completing all of the tasks expected. The team felt they were constantly nagging their students to "get busy and be quiet" the moment they walked in the door. What was up? The teachers knew that *they* were psyched to walk into their classrooms every morning. Why weren't the kids feeling it?

Reflecting across their pod's table one morning, Faith, Abby, Katie, and Ashley tried to puzzle it out. Faith suggested: "Why not think about how *we* start the day, how we get ourselves revved up? Maybe we'll notice something that we could do differently with the kids." So they started to talk about their own morning ritual. Arriving around the same time, coffee in hand, they would meet in the pod, giving family news updates, sharing pictures on phones, chatting about TV shows, going over their plans for the kids' day, gathering up materials, and finally, marching down the hall together to their special wing of the building. After reflecting on this, the fifth-grade team staff made some big changes to the first fifteen minutes of the day.

A few months later, I found myself in the fifth-grade wing at Eason. At 8:15 a.m. sharp, the buses arrived, just up a gentle slope from the door. The kids scrambled to their homerooms and threw off their backpacks. Immediately, in all four rooms, loud music started playing and the kids broke into dancing. Yes, dancing. And within moments, almost every kid in Faith's room was up and moving (check out Figures 2.8 and 2.9).

"Mrs. Shellabarger, can we do a conga line?" asked a girl wearing Crayola pajamas (today was also PJ day). Faith, who was dancing herself, answered, "Sure," and about twelve kids grabbled one another's hips and snaked off down the hall to greet their friends in the other three classrooms.

Although I couldn't be in all four rooms at once, I saw a rich variety of dancing. When the conga line got to Katie's room, they dissolved into the "Cupid Shuffle," a line dance under way there (kids prefer the radio edit; me too, and I downloaded it as soon as I got back to my hotel). Occasionally, a kid would bust out a special dance move for others to watch and applaud. Down the hall, the more athletic "Cha Cha Slide" was happening, a good chance for me to rest, in the guise of taking pictures.

Figure 2.8 Fifth graders working on dance moves during greeting ritual

Figure 2.9 Faith and her kids practice the moves for a new slide dance.

As I followed (unable to resist jiggling a little myself) I saw lots of hugs, high-fives, and fist bumps between many kids, boys and girls equally. It felt like a sports team warming up for a playoff game or a theatre company getting psyched for opening night.

Later, the teachers explained to me that, among other things, the dance party was designed as a *greeting ritual*, a chance for kids to say hello and swap energy with all their friends before the day began (your neighborhood pals aren't necessarily in the same homeroom). This mimicked what the teachers themselves did together each day before school, greeting and pumping each other up for the day ahead. The kids decided to name their daily dance-a-thon "Peace, Love, and Understanding, Inc." Clearly they grasped the intent at a heart level.

This thoughtful strategy also recognized the developmental needs of young adolescents. In too many middle schools, adults spend the whole day trying to tamp down kids' energy, to bottle it up, to keep the lid on and the cork in. Faith, Katie, Ashley, and Abby thought it made more sense to let kids jump and dance for fifteen minutes, getting physically active right at the start of the day. As the dance party became a daily occurrence, teachers discovered that the greeting ritual worked for them as well: this casual, unstructured time helped them to build stronger rapport and relationships with individual kids.

If you have been thinking "my kids could never handle this," team member Abby Schmitz sympathizes with you. "I think the best way to prevent crazy behavior and to make this idea a hit is student involvement from the beginning. We let kids pick the music, with the understanding that it must be school appropriate. While free-styling is always welcome, we also ask the kids which group-oriented dances they think would be fun."

Another way to begin this soft start would be with the music and greeting time, but no dancing at first. Just legalize kids' ability to socialize before schoolwork starts. I'd keep the idea of visiting other classrooms that are joining in this ritual.

POINT OUT

"In most classrooms, kids suggested Cha-Cha Slide and the Cupid Shuffle. Line dances are nice because many students already know what the moves are, and if they don't, they can just get behind someone who knows the dance and practice it. I have even played a YouTube video with people doing the dance so students can feel comfortable participating. In my class of twenty-six, I truly have about twenty-three kids who participate every time. They just LOVE it. The other kids are comfortable just watching as well."

Not everyone dances the whole time, or at all. It is fine to watch and talk. But the norm is: no doing homework or web surfing alone. This is a social time for the community; there will be plenty of quiet, solo work time throughout the day. In fact, one such opportunity comes up in *the next fifteen minutes*—as the kids transition to one of the gentlest soft starts I've ever seen (see pages 72–75).

Back in Faith's room, a group of kids were doing a full-throated sing-along with Journey's catchy-cheesy anthem "Don't Stop Believing." Because I am old, I knew the words, and was lip-synching right along. But these eleven-year-olds? This tune was a hit in 1981, *before most of their parents were born*. After the fade, I asked one pony-tailed girl who had been belting it out: "How do you know those words?"

Samantha looked at me dreamily, adjusting her hair tie. "I don't know, we just do."

We all want a highly collaborative, friendly, respectful, and supportive classroom. First, of course, we wish this for our human living together. But we also want to lead kids into challenging and collaborative learning investigations all year long—and for that, we need a high level of trust, collaboration, partnership, and commitment.

To create this inquiry-friendly climate, there are steps we already take, especially at the beginning of the school year. But as I hope this chapter has shown, building that community isn't just a first-week-of-school thing—we have to keep deepening and sustaining our relationships with students week by week, month by month. And, on the very bright side, the world abounds with lessons, structures, and activities that we can use to undertake this necessary and delightful work. We want kids to find their school irresistible, welcoming, and positive. We will know this is working when they line up at the door early every morning, dying to get in (Figures 2.10–2.12).

Figure 2.10 Kids waiting to get into Eason Elementary School

Figure 2.11 Yay, we're in!

Figure 2.12 Dance party starts in five minutes!

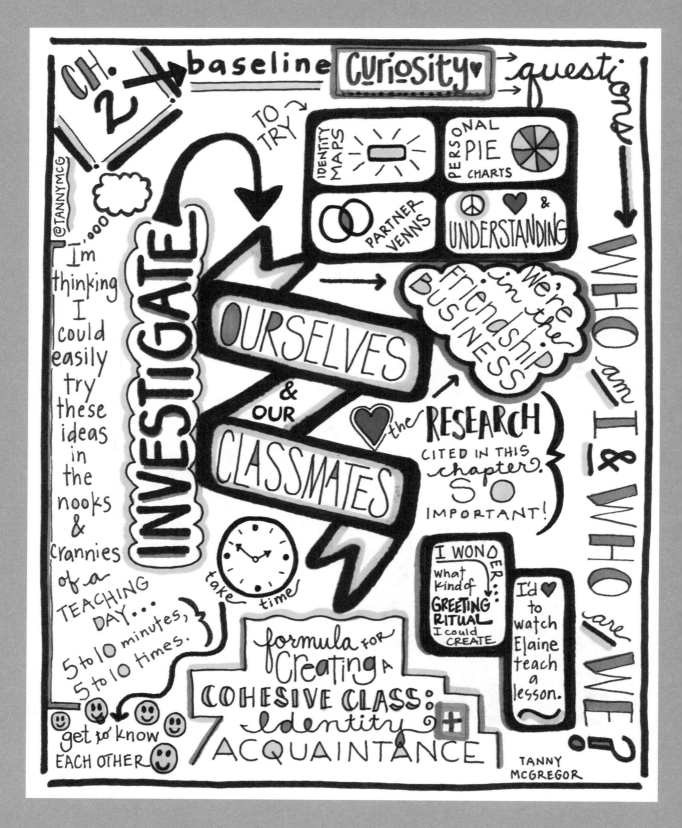

Supportive classrooms are not just mysteriously dealt out; they can be *made* from the raw materials that are delivered to us each fall. We can take affirmative steps from the start of the year to dramatically raise the odds of growing a collaborative group of students who can take responsibility for challenging and cooperative inquiries all year long.

3

Capture and Honor Kids' Questions

Why

If we are going to build our instruction out of kids' questions—whether these arise from a required curriculum or emerge from children's free-range curiosity—we need a system. To create a culture of questioning and investigation, we need to solicit and record topics kids wonder about, make time for them, pursue them, and keep track of kids' efforts along the way.

What We Might Say to Kids

"What are some topics that you are curious about? Let's all make lists of some things we would like to learn more about—inside or outside of school. You can keep a list of your own questions, and we can also list them here on a chart for everyone to see."

how Long It Might Take

Students post their questions and wonders every day, either in their own notebook or on a public chart. This can take from one to five minutes. Then, at another designated time of the week, some minutes are set aside for kids to pursue questions from the wall or from their personal notes.

'm visiting Micki Schumacher's first-grade room in Waukee, Iowa. While class is in session, a girl quietly gets up, walks to the back of the room, and places a sticky note on a chart hanging there. I realize she is posting her question beside a picture of herself, which is stuck to the chart along with every other face in first grade. "Why do zebras have strips?" reads Angie's question (shown in Figure 3.1). She has already returned to her seat and rejoined the class at work.

Angie has just posted on a wonder wall (see Figure 3.2), one of many tools teachers have developed to store students' hot topics and burning questions for future investigation.

Most inquiry teachers around the country show kids how to set up some kind of journal or notebook to record all their questions, thinking, research, and information. Variations abound.

Figure 3.1 Angie posts a wonder.

Figure 3.2 Wonder wall in Eason Elementary School first grade

At Eason Elementary School, kids include "moon shots" in their learning logs—innovative, earth-shaking ideas they hope to pursue. At Columbine Elementary, Brad Buhrow has a colorful wonder wall at kids' eye level, surrounded by writing supplies. His first graders post actively and he checks the wall contantly during the seams in the day. When there's time, Brad will leave an answer or suggestion on a sticky note. Periodically, he will start a whole new wonder wall with a curricular theme like "What is a habitat?" or "What is a scientist?" and do a minilesson right beside the wall to introduce it to kids.

Try This

It's said that curiosity is an itch we love to scratch. Let's see what makes you itchy. Make a commitment to spend forty-eight hours jotting down the questions and wonders that arise as you move though your life. This means being attentive to events, people, scenes, stories, or other input that grabs your interest, that makes you want to learn more, dig deeper, and understand what's going on. My guess is you'll notice how many things activate your brain's "wonder center" every day, even if most are quickly forgotten in the rush of events. You'll need a portable note-taking device for this constant monitoring—your phone, a journal, or a back pocket notepad. The resulting list will be the perfect document to show your kids as you encourage them to notice and capture their own curiosity questions.

At Duke School, sixth graders make "noticing books" to bring with them on summer break. These mutipupose journals are collectors for reading notes, souvenirs, journal entries, phtotographs, used tickets, and personal artifacts from summer adventures (see Figure 3.3). When kids come back to school in the fall, their noticing books become a source for deep and thoughtful "what I did last summer" conversations. So powerful are these logs, teachers told me, that some kids go on to voluntarily maintain them throughout the school year.

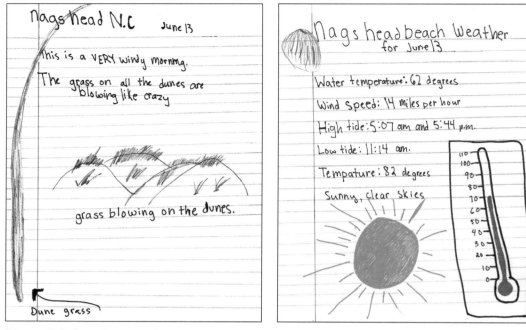

Figure 3.3 Sample page of a "noticing book" by a Duke School student

So what do we mean by *honoring* the questions? We:

- actively and regularly solicit kids' wonders
- allow ourselves to be interrupted
- are open to being amazed
- create a keeping place for kids' questions, return to it often, and keep it fresh
- make time for children to pursue their questions
- model how we find answers ourselves
- create sharing opportunities within and beyond the class

And then (a little harder task), how do we provide time for children to work on their questions? Let's look at four ways teachers evoke, capture, and honor kids' inquiry questions throughout the school year, and find time for children to pursue the topics they've chosen—even into the summer.

SET UP AND MAINTAIN A WONDER WALL
When we wonder about something, we need to know more

Kari Ridolfi, kindergarten teacher
at Burley School

Kindergarten teacher Kari Ridolfi uses a wonder wall in her classroom to provide her students a way to ask questions, seek answers, and validate their curiosity (see Figure 3.4). The wonder wall is located in the students' writing center, where they have access to writing tools and a variety of sticky notes. Throughout the week, students add their wonders to the wall. Wonders may come from questions that pop up during independent reading or from lingering questions at the conclusion of a lesson. Thursdays and Fridays, the students visit the wonder wall as a whole group to seek answers to their questions.

While the teacher does do some preparation for the wonder research, the students take full ownership during the wonder workshop to read articles and images, interact with artifacts, and record their new learning to share with classmates.

Figure 3.4 Wonder wall in Kari Ridolfi's kindergarten at Burley School

Notice how Kari devotes a piece of each day of the week to supporting the wonder wall: three days of generating questions and two days of finding answers to selected questions.

POINT OUT

Monday, Tuesday, and Wednesday children fill the wonder wall with things that they are curious about. Just recently, these were some of the kids' burning questions:

- If I swallow a seed, will it grow in my stomach?
- How did the first person on Earth get here?
- What is the most famous book ever written?
- How far can a spider monkey jump?
- How many links would it take to measure our classroom?
- How are dinosaur fossils created?
- Were dragons real or make-believe?
- Do tornadoes come to Chicago?
- Are super powers real?
- How does a praying mantis eat?

As students add wonders, Kari groups similar topics together. For example, if there are several questions about dinosaurs, she'll move them to a shared space on the wonder wall. This helps to keep the wonder wall organized and track similar student curiosities.

On Thursdays, students visit the wonder wall as a group. They read aloud wonders that are on the wall, recognize similarities, and decide which wonders they are most curious about as a class. After narrowing the choices down to five or six, Kari will write each chosen wonder at the top of a fresh piece of chart paper. Students then have an opportunity to sign up on the chart for which wonder they'd like to investigate, thus forming groups.

POINT OUT

While this structure helps Kari place kids into small teams, it also sets up *individual inquiries* very well. Kids can work solo if they wish on any question from the week-long wonder wall extravaganza.

Once students have gathered into their teams, they scour the classroom library for resources, do searches for online information, and make a list of artifacts that could be helpful to their investigation. They start to create a resource basket for their inquiry. After the first session concludes, Kari will gather and create additional resources to add to each group's basket—printing images for children to analyze, retyping articles to create age-appropriate resources, and collecting toys and artifacts all become part of the weekly routine.

On Friday, children get back into their wonder groups. Using sticky notes, chart paper, construction paper, and other writing materials, students get to work. They take turns reading resources aloud and recording new information. Each member of the group is responsible for contributing one piece of new learning. Students choose to write facts, draw pictures, or create diagrams to share thinking. Kari circles around the group, monitoring collaboration and troubleshooting with children when they arrive at any roadblocks.

Once the research phase has concluded, the students meet back on the carpet where kids in each wonder group have the opportunity to share their new learning. The wonder posters are then hung around the room for the students to marvel at and to celebrate their weekly wonder workshop.

To conclude their session, Kari and the students work on the maintenance of the wonder wall. Several wonders are read aloud and the group decides whether these are still lingering questions. Sometimes wonders are removed because answers have already been found or students have lost interest in the questions. By doing a weekly cleanse, it allows space for all the following weeks' wonders to be posted as the curiosity cycle continues. Figure 3.5 shows another variation of a wonder wall, this one from Duke School.

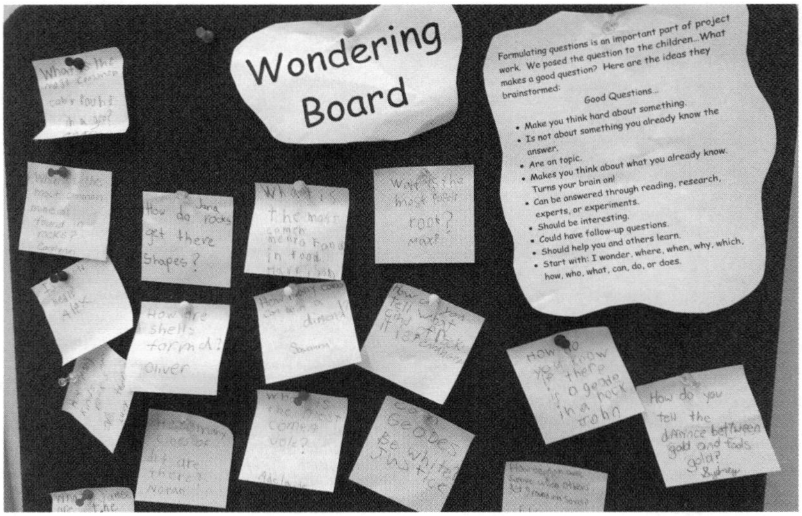

Figure 3.5 Wondering board from Duke School

USE IDEA NOTEBOOKS
Why can't I see my eyes?

Megan Dixon, second-grade teacher at Glenwood School

Megan, whose terrible feet we learned about in Chapter 1, is a connoisseur of student questions. The rocket fuel of her second-grade classroom is kid curiosity. Sometimes children's wonders pop out in questions that can be insightful, funny, and just plain strange.

> Do you have to be Irish to find a leprechaun?
>
> Why can't I see my eyes?
>
> How do we know we're actually real and not a dream?
>
> Why is everything made in China?
>
> Why are there so many names for poop?
>
> What do race car drivers do when they have to pee?

Megan's class maintains a vibrant Wonder Window (see Figure 3.6), similar to Kari Ridolfi's wonder wall, but she and her students also keep personal Idea Notebooks. Megan explains:

Figure 3.6 Megan Dixon's Wonder Window "breathes curiosity into our classroom."

Hearing and recording students' questions is the first step in honoring their curiosity. But it can't stop there. What really matters is making time in the day—every day—to allow students to investigate their own wonders and curiosities. I have always believed that if my students could pose their own "burning questions," the ones that they are most passionate about, I would no longer be the keeper of knowledge, the question answerer, the decider. Instead, all of us would be responsible for investigating the questions, sharing the teaching and learning with each other. To me, this kind of engagement is not only authentic, but joyful.

The Wonder Window breathes curiosity into our classroom.

In addition to posting on the Wonder Window, our second graders consistently capture their curiosities in Idea Notebooks. Beginning on the first day of school, students notice me carrying my Idea Notebook and jotting things down throughout the day. [See Figure 3.7.] Modeling my curious life involves consistently using my notebook and making my thinking visible to students.

Our notebooks typically include two sections, one with writing ideas and drafts, and the other a place to jot questions and investigate curiosities. The writing ideas section includes a heart map, writer's eye, authority list, top 10 lists, favorite lines and quotes from books, experiments in writer's craft, noteworthy words, phrases, and sentences, minilessons, and drafts. Students often tuck letters, photographs, and other memories in their notebooks to use during writer's workshop.

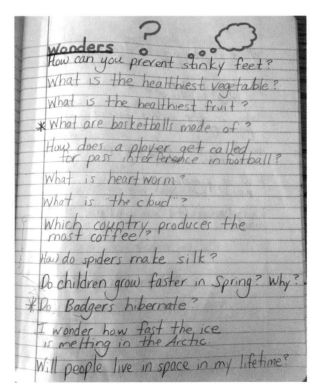

Figure 3.7 Page from teacher Megan Dixon's Idea Notebook

This is an example of how you can coordinate student-directed inquiry along with other adopted curricula, such as the *Units of Study* programs from Lucy Calkins et al. (2013, 2016).

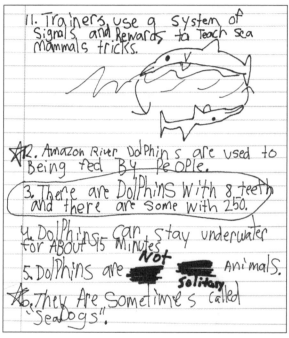

Figure 3.8 Page from a student's Idea Notebook

The second section of the Idea Notebook is a place to think, wonder, and question (see Figure 3.7 for a teacher example and 3.8 for a student page). My students fondly name this section of their notebook the "think tank," "curiosity corner," or "imagination station." Here, kids have a special space to notice and note, listen and collect, wonder and play with language as writers and thinkers. In their portable think tank, students gather questions and write down curiosities throughout the school day. When we gather on the carpet, students bring their notebooks to write ideas and questions that emerge from our class meeting or an interactive read-aloud, or while we navigate websites like Wonderopolis, Newsela, or National Geographic.

Sometimes these notebook opportunities are intentionally planned. For example, when reading Gail Gibbons' text *Knights in Shining Armor,* students actively generated and recorded questions during specific stopping points I'd used in the text. These questions served as a launching point for a mini-inquiry into the era of knights and castles. Students drew maps based on narrative descriptions of castles, intensely interacted with informational text by co-constructing their own labels and text features, and wrote new learning and additional questions in—where else?—their Idea Notebooks.

Other times, the use of the notebooks is completely student driven and emerges from an authentic purpose. When one of their classmates went to Germany, the other students had many questions about what it was like there and what Patrick might be doing.

How long did it take Patrick to fly there?

Do they have big cities?

Is soccer popular in Germany?

What does German sound like?

Seizing this opportunity to engage in authentic inquiry, I asked students to write their questions in their notebooks, share ideas with one another, and brainstorm resources they might need to answer these questions. A short time later, we had gathered multiple texts from our library and maps from our classroom, pulled up several websites, and placed large world atlases on the carpet to explore their questions and record what they learned.

Throughout the year, my students often engage in longer-term inquiry about topics that begin as a single question. The students and I frequently spend time reviewing the questions and ideas in our notebooks. Oftentimes, I'll model my own process of going back into my notebook and rediscovering something I had forgotten or noticing patterns in my questions. I'll also highlight ones I'm still really curious about or check others I have investigated. After one of these modeling opportunities, Vanessa—one of our wildly curious students—noticed that many of her questions were about the brain. Then, over the course of several weeks, Vanessa independently checked out numerous books from our school library about the brain, studied many texts from our classroom library, watched videos, and took notes in her Idea Notebook about her learning. She was growing her brain by writing about it, no doubt!

We all know that kids enter school naturally curious and inquisitive. They arrive full of questions about their classmates and teachers, the subjects they're learning, and the whole wide world. It's also often acknowledged that kids' curiosity somehow disappears by about fourth grade. By using tools like Wonder Windows and Idea Notebooks, we keep kids' curiosity alive and well as they move up through the grades.

IGNITE COMMUNITY CURIOSITY

Engaging families in inquiry on back-to-school night

Steve Newcomer, principal at Glenwood School

When I became principal at Glenwood three years ago, the whole faculty gathered to collaboratively create a "heartbeat statement" to represent what makes our school unique. Here's what we came up with:

We are a collaborative community of learners who:

- *nurture curiosity* and *wonder*,
- *encourage* each other to *be our best*, and
- *celebrate* getting *smarter* every day.

We monitor this heartbeat every day.

As we got ready for the start of school last year, we were feeling pretty good about the opening days. But one last topic of concern kept coming up: How do we make sure our school *parents* understand what all this inquiry-based learning is like, so they are able to make that curiosity connection at home?

As we planned for our Welcome Back Open House, we decided to spice up this traditional event by evoking every family's curiosity. Someone pitched the idea of each family receiving a blank "passport" upon entering the building and framing the evening's events as an exciting adventure. We set up a series of "countries"—stations that each family would visit to learn about aspects of Glenwood, receiving a "visa stamp" each time. This helped energize families to accomplish all the normal chores of an open house (getting school pictures taken, dropping off supplies, learning about the library, and signing up for lunch plans). Once their passport was filled up with stamps, the family's last stop was the cafeteria, where they met our awesome PTO and slurped some ice cream.

Of course, we wanted some of the passport stations to explicitly model our heartbeat. What could better represent "living a curious life" than to have wonder walls standing at kid level, right outside every classroom door? Each poster had a heading saying, "What do you want to learn in _____ grade this year?" with a convenient tray of markers below. [See Figure 3.9.] So, before they even set foot in their new classrooms, every student had a chance to jot down their wonders—their personal learning agenda—for the grade they were beginning.

For the parents, often with "extra" children in tow (or in arms), there was a place to record their curiosity questions, too. Deb Zaffiro, our instructional coach, constructed another passport stop for parents: a giant Family Wonder Wall outside of our library. At this station, staff members helped families to write their own wonderings on the board. Among the entries were questions like:

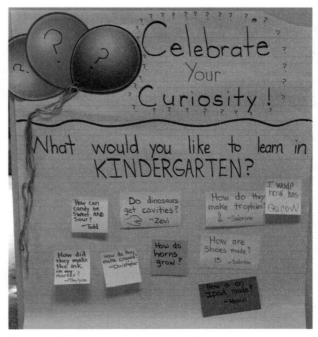

Figure 3.9 One of the wonder walls on every classroom door

How do people make animated movies?

What year was Glenwood built?

Why can't summer be longer?

What are we going to get in the new playground?

How many books are there in the school?

What is Play-Doh made of?

Why does Mr. Stengerwold like Pearl Jam so much?

Are lady bugs toxic?

I'm curious about the human body. . . .

The Family Wonder Wall remained in place for the first few weeks of school, and students would often point out what their parents and/or families had written on the wall.

A hundred and eighty school days later, as the year is winding down, wonder walls are still up and actively used in every classroom, from junior K through fifth grade—and they are ever-changing with the wide-ranging curiosities of our students.

Not only have wonder walls been consistently used in our classrooms all year long, one also hangs in the teachers' lounge. We've honored our own culture goal that "students and teachers will regularly show multiple forms of evidence of living a curious life." The whole faculty has been using our wonder wall to get to know each other better, to share personal news and enjoy some high-fives, to build supportive relationships, and to live out the practice we have been growing with our children every day.

That sad old assumption that school beats the curiosity out of kids by fourth grade might have been true once. But when we honor kids' questions like these teachers do, we can set that worry aside. As I mentioned in the introduction, new research shows that we have a "curiosity switch" in our brains that, once flipped on, gives learners the superpower of self-sustaining, intrinsically motivated research. Displaying children's specific questions all around the room, on charts, in idea notebooks, on the walls and windows, keeps the current flowing and energizes learning.

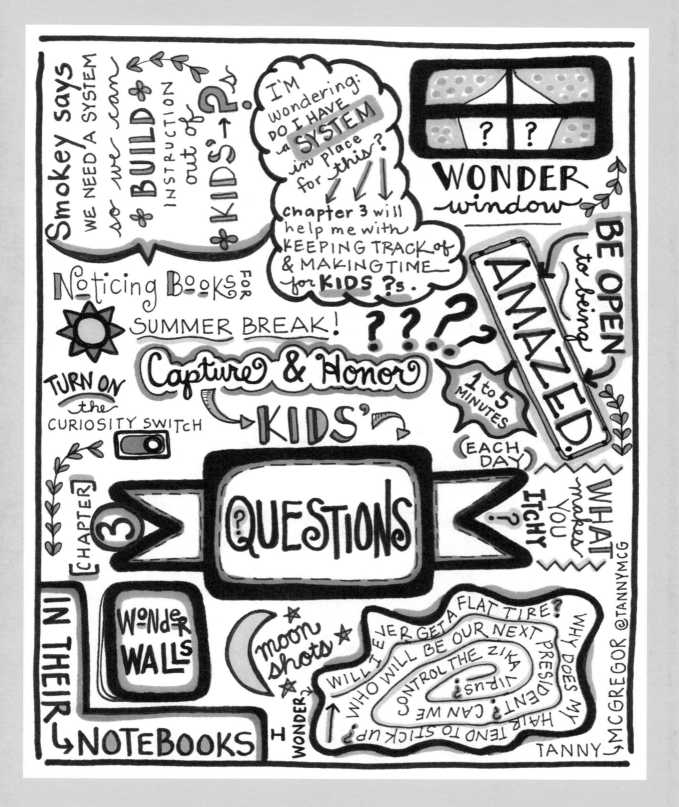

4

Begin the Day with Soft Starts

why

We don't have to teach the whole class from the opening bell. The first chunk of the day/class can be personal choice time—quiet, industrious, and maybe even shoeless. When we let kids find their own way into the day, we activate their curiosity and sense of self-direction, mind-sets that serve learners well in the formal inquiries that follow.

what

We Might Say to Kids

"Good morning, friends. I have an idea. Let's take the first few minutes of each day this week and have everyone use that time to pursue a curiosity topic of their own. What could be some choices? Yes, independent reading would be a great idea. What else? Researching insects with a buddy would be fine, too."

how

Long It Might Take

Ten to fifteen minutes per day. Try it for one week; it's potentially useful all year.

When I arrived to visit Sara Ahmed's classroom one morning, I was surprised to see the kids' shoes neatly stacked up just outside the door. Further into the room, I could see students scattered all around, lying on the floor, draped over couches, sitting back to back at desks. Most were reading a book or tablet, others were writing notes in a journal, and a few were talking quietly. Sara was on the floor reading too.

I slipped off my shoes, tiptoed in, and began reading the *New York Times* on my phone. As I settled in, I found myself enjoying this interval of calm, a respite from my frantic travel and this tightly packed day. After a few minutes, Sara quietly announced, "Everyone, please grab your journals and meet me on the rug." And that was it: a soft start. As the kids gathered promptly on the rug, they were alert, attentive, and full of energy.

In the customary school day, we teach from "bell to bell," always spending "time on task" and never "wasting" a minute. But why? Do kids really benefit from living in overdrive, with a nonstop onslaught of tasks that reproduces the worst aspects of today's frantic workplaces? When we begin handing out worksheets or spewing information the second kids walk through our door, are we contributing to what Stanford psychologist Emma Seppala (2016) calls "toxic stress"? It's worth considering what is really the best way for kids to begin their school day.

Try This

Thinking back on your own elementary school experience, write down the names of your teachers by grade level. I know—as if! Unless you have a superhuman memory (or are in your twenties), these names won't all pop into your head—but jot as many as you can. If you are like me, you might remember a face or a feeling but not the name. Draw or write those attributes. Warning: Many times, memories of your middle or high school teachers will intrude on this experiment, but try to rule those out for now.

Now comes the fun part. See if you can remember how any of those teachers *started the day*. What activities came first? Perhaps:

the Pledge of Allegiance
the National Anthem
a prayer
play time
a teacher-directed lesson
seatwork
a class meeting
a greeting ritual
music or songs
movement
a read-aloud
free time
silent reading
show and tell
a bell ringer

I hope these possibilities help trigger your memory. As you ponder, you may come up with general memories of how the day typically began in the schools you attended. But maybe there also was one teacher who started the day in a really unusual or interesting way. What details can you recall about that?

On your own or with colleagues, reflect on how your childhood school days typically began. How engaging or energizing was each way of launching into the morning? Talk about the "outlier" teachers, if you remembered any whose day-beginning routine was unique. Finally, think about the first ten or fifteen minutes of the school days you are in charge of now. Are you pleased with the routine, or looking for fresh ideas?

Nobody seems to know where soft starts came from—but the name makes sense. Not rigid, but gentle, individualized, and peaceful beginnings, driven by personal choice, not ordained by someone else's agenda or requirements. If kids begin the day gradually and on their own recognizance, they will feel safe and in control, and can later glide into challenging inquiry work more smoothly and with more genuine engagement. Looked at over a whole day of school, a fifteen-minute soft start is an investment in the overall seven-hour outcome. Kids will accomplish more "net learning" if they start that day in the driver's seat.

What about morning meeting?

Many teachers have an established morning meeting, often patterned after the model from Responsive Classroom (2016). According to the organization:

> Morning Meeting is an engaging way to start each day, build a strong sense of community, and set children up for success socially and academically. Each morning, students and teachers gather together in a circle for twenty to thirty minutes and interact with one another during four purposeful components:
>
> 1. **Greeting:** Students and teachers greet one other by name and practice offering hospitality.
>
> 2. **Sharing:** Students share information about important events in their lives. Listeners often offer empathetic comments or ask clarifying questions.
>
> 3. **Group Activity:** Everyone participates in a brief, lively activity that fosters group cohesion and helps students practice social and academic skills (for example, reciting a poem, dancing, singing, or playing a game that reinforces social or academic skills).
>
> 4. **Morning Message:** Students read and interact with a short message written by their teacher. The message is crafted to help students focus on the work they'll do in school that day. (Responsive Classroom 2016)

Many of the teachers you are meeting in this book also conduct a morning meeting. You may especially see a family resemblance between morning meeting and some of the soft starts in this chapter. Both models are completely harmonious and can easily be combined. The one consistent difference is that the soft starts aim to let kids begin the day by following their own curiosity, while morning meetings are usually a teacher-led whole-class activity.

Now let's look at four different models of soft starts from teachers around the country. Kids can choose these morning openers in the moment, or teachers can offer open-ended structures every day—or different choices each day of the week. Soft starts allow kids to work alone, join in deep partnerships, or involve the whole class. As you will see in each model, the kids are actively inquiring—looking into books, investigating topics, constructing objects, and even creating teams, but without a standard school *assignment*.

PUT PLAY FIRST
Purposeful play and soft starts

Sue Musson, Lyndsey Popham, Debbie McLachlan, Heather Isham, and **Hayley Abell**, kindergarten and first-grade teachers at Virginia Chance School

Expanded version on website

In the recent years of test- and data-driven school reform, many teachers have complained that all forms of play, playfulness, and fun were being strictly curtailed. We have felt this most acutely in the primary grades, where once-treasured periods of play (recess, sand table, dress-up corner) were subtracted from the day to make room for more academics, test prep, and testing. But now, play is back, big-time. There are emerging research studies and a buzz of teacher talk around the centrality of play in the cognitive and social development of children—and not just the youngest ones.

One of the most striking of these recent studies comes from Peter Gray, author of *Free to Learn*. He reminds us that among most animals, definitely including us primates, free play is the norm among young ones. This play serves as a rehearsal for real-life activities such as hunting and stalking (think lion cubs), but also happens for the inherent joy of it. Gray also studied human hunter-gatherer tribes, and found that in almost every such culture, the children were allowed complete freedom to play. Why did young humans play so actively? "They did it," Gray explains, "because it was fun and because something deep inside them, the result of aeons of natural selection, urged them to play at culturally appropriate activities so they would become skilled and knowledgeable adults" (2013).

The importance of play is actively on the minds of the thoughtful teachers at Virginia Chance School in Louisville, Kentucky. It was a shortage of play that set them searching for another way to begin their K–1 days. Sue Musson and colleagues pick up the story:

> We developed "soft starts" at Chance School knowing that the curriculum is everything that happens between a child's arrival at school until his or her dismissal in the afternoon. Our K–1 team wanted all parts of our day to be purposeful, meaningful, and attuned to both individual children's needs and the needs of the group. But at the time, the first half-hour of school was not working for us as teachers or for our kids in their classrooms.
>
> Previously, this time was designated for free writing. The children came in, sorted their belongings, signed in, and then quietly found their writing journals. However, we noticed the students' unmet desire to greet one another, and many of them didn't even seem to enjoy this writing time. We wanted writing not to feel like a dull task, but to be a powerful tool for reflection, expression, and communication. We also wanted kids to cultivate relationships and be a strong learning community. Further, we noticed that our daily schedule did not always allow for an unstructured yet purposeful play or discovery time, and we believed this was very important to provide for our age group.

POINT OUT

Maybe when you look into your classroom, you can see one element that isn't working right or that doesn't justify the time it gets. This could be an activity, a schedule, a program. That's where we often find an opening for change, and the teachers from Chance did.

Research has taught us how play allows children to practice prosocial behaviors, ignite their imagination and creativity, explore the world around them, and engage in reasoning. So we decided to try soft starts—beginning the school day with an open-ended, playful, exploratory time for both relationship building and child-centered learning. We hoped that this would fill in what kids seemed to be missing, and also prime their brains for the rest of the day.

First we needed to change our classroom environments to be more conducive to student-initiated exploration, investigation, and creation. We moved furniture around until we had distinct learning areas: a studio space for writing and art, a construction area for building, a Peace Corner for times a child wants to be alone, a sensory table for tactile exploration and imagination, and shelves for "invitations," materials we chose to invite the children to apply or to extend their knowledge, abilities, or imagination in some way.

Once our rooms were rearranged, we began adding materials. For example, in the block area, we placed two sets of high-quality wooden blocks and a sundry supply of accessories, such as blue and green glass stones, creek rocks, sticks, animal and insect figurines, and clipboards for drawing block designs. In the studio space, we put an abundance of art supplies, including oil pastels, watercolor paints, black felt-tip pens, crayons, markers, tape, glue, scissors, colored pencils, an assortment of paper, and envelopes. We also added other materials for open-ended use: flowers, raffia, yarn, popsicle sticks, corks, and beads. We included a big tub full of recyclables for the children to create with, which overflowed with paper towel tubes, bottle caps, tissue boxes, clean cottage cheese containers—and another big tub full of fabric scraps.

These spaces were intended for the children to have creative freedom to explore different materials and use them in whatever ways their imaginations inspired. And they have. Those learning areas have been teeming with imagination and transformation since we began our soft start.

For just one example: though children often play alone, we've also seen the spontaneous emergence of group projects. In the picture here [Figure 4.1], a small group of children brought out building materials to the large area rug so they could work in a bigger space. More children joined them until they had an imaginative story unraveling about a magical kitty and dog world. They explored these open-ended materials by independently and collaboratively building and then creating a story together. Another team of kids who became fascinated by a peacock feather they found among the soft start materials later went out on the playground and organized their own circus,

Figure 4.1 Harris, Bowie, and Stella created a winter tobogganing scene during their soft start, using blocks, greens, yarn, and toy animals.

Figure 4.2 Student journal about soft start project

On the playground, we Made a srcis and I BaLinsr Sophia's Peecoc FeThere. On MY hed

starring Katy, who could balance the feather on her head for all to see! When free play time was up, the kids eagerly grabbed their journals and wrote about their explorations [Figure 4.2].

MEET WITH PAIR COACHES
AM–PM buddies support each other all day

Sarah Van Lieshout, third-grade teacher at Glenwood School

A recent schedule change at Glenwood opened up the possibility for teachers to rethink the start of their day. The district adjusted arrival procedures to allow students to come to their classrooms fifteen minutes before the first bell rings. This means that students slowly trickle into the rooms, making it possible to start the day with real, meaningful conversations instead of the old hustle and bustle to get ready to immediately go to gym or music. Sarah explains how she seized the opportunity:

Prior to this change, my students had been egging me on to help them create "classroom clubs." This was their idea of a homeroom "support group" to celebrate, share, and encourage each other at the beginning and end of every day. They had been convincing me. I could see some benefits if support group members would really help each other monitor personal goals, provide encouragement, and build closer relationships (and hopefully discourage some clique-like behavior that was beginning to develop). But I didn't know where we would find the time. Now, with an extra fifteen minutes suddenly added to our morning, we could try it.

As we become more and more trusting of our kids, their focus, and their work ethic, it becomes easier to simply say yes to something that kids want to try.

POINT OUT

It turned out that many of the kids were thinking of having just one partner or buddy, not so much a multimember support group. I thought this was a more workable structure, too. But I didn't want kids just pairing up with their best friend since preschool, and some others being left out. So I formed the pairs randomly, using "The Hat," an easy list randomizer on the web. Spotting a couple of potentially bad combos, I rearranged those pairs, and then announced the matchups to the kids. I feared some pushback when I announced the pairings, but kids took to their new partners. It seemed that they really had been interested in the idea of supporting classmates, not just in hanging with a preselected pal [check out one pair in Figure 4.3].

I did not set any rigid expectations, except that partners should remain focused on each other during the start and end of each day. The kids could talk, read, or research together during our soft start. (Yes, we made a little room for an afternoon "soft finish" too, just before bus time.)

Figure 4.3 Partners look out for each other all day.

The relationships that have bloomed among our soft start buddies have been outstanding! For some reason, these special partners are eagerly accountable to each other throughout the school day. In the halls, I've overhead passing buddies saying: "Did you remember your math homework?" or "Did you have a good time at recess?" I've also watched as pairs naturally evolved their own traditions for starting each day together. Some AM–PM buddies are coauthoring a book; another pair shares their favorite parts of a book they are reading; many partnerships research a question they are wondering about and swap facts. Although I encouraged that these parts of the day should be highly collaborative, some buddies also choose to explore ideas independently, but still sit side by side.

All I gave them was fifteen minutes to explore what mattered to them and they came up with the rest.

I love the way these motivated students are choosing to use their soft start to read, write, and investigate. What has been most impressive is that my kids needed minimal guidance or structure to make this time valuable. All I gave them was fifteen minutes to explore what mattered to them and they came up with the rest.

They haven't needed constant reminders of the expectations or guidelines—they were ready for this! What I savor most about this structure for starting each day is that the focus is on the personal relationships and the fresh ideas that naturally develop from the collaboration process itself, not on a required product or outcome.

Clearly, collaboration, friendliness, and support are front and center in the AM–PM buddy model. But this is still an inquiry project—one in which kids are investigating a topic called *each other*. Remember that Sarah paired the kids randomly; she kept the lifelong buddies apart so that students had to build a relationship with somebody they didn't know well. Of course, combined with other acquaintance-building activities throughout the year, Sarah is mindfully creating a climate in which everyone is ready to work with any classmate without hesitation or resistance.

DEFINE A DAILY SOFT START THEME
Monday is "Weekend Wrap-Up," Tuesday is . . .

Julie Eisenhauer, fifth-grade teacher at Glenwood School

Some teachers create soft starts that give kids complete freedom to explore, well, almost anything. Others like to provide a bit more structure within which kids can wonder, while making sure the whole class is nudged into a curious frame of mind. Monday through Friday, Julie Eisenhauer welcomes her fifth graders to school with a different soft start theme. Each day she allows fifteen to thirty minutes to offer kids a provocative, open-ended stimulus for their exploration, thought, and sharing.

Monday: To soft-start the week, Julie's kids have a "Weekend Wrap-Up." At one level, this simply legalizes something the kids do naturally, but bringing it from the hallways into the classroom ensures that everyone gets to share and feel included. Immediately after morning announcements, students gather in pairs on the carpet. To begin, Julie will sometimes do a two-minute minilesson on working with a partner (using your indoor voice, giving the speaker your eyes). The rest of the time belongs to the kids. They plunge in with their buddies, sharing news of sleepovers, recapping their sporting events, replaying video game triumphs, or just recalling their outdoor play. As time runs down, Julie asks volunteer pairs to share highlights with the class. This comfortable ritual not only gives kids a chance to learn about each other's out-of-school lives, it also provides vital practice in taking turns, listening actively, speaking up, and other social-academic skills that will be called upon the rest of the day.

Tuesday: Next comes "Talking Tuesdays," for which Julie distributes (via email and/or hard copy) a fascinating nonfiction "Article of the Week" (Gallagher 2016). Many times, she chooses an article that will fit into an upcoming curricular unit but that, for now, can simply be enjoyed and puzzled over. As they come into the room, students settle down and read today's piece, marking important, interesting, or puzzling details. Next, they list some questions they have about the topic.

One recent week, the article was about the wooly mammoth, which had ranged through the local Wisconsin habitat until the last ice age. This led to curious questions about mammoths and elephants:

- So if wooly mammoths had fur, what do elephants have?

- I know elephants have thick skin—did mammoths?

- Learning about mammoths having small ears to prevent heat loss, it reminds me of jackrabbits in the desert. Do they have long ears for a reason?

Wednesday: On "Wonderopolis Wednesdays," Julie assigns students a "Wonder of the Day" from the famed question-generating website. Students read or listen to the article, watch the video clip, and record their lingering questions in their Wonder Notebook. Then it's time to inquire: kids can spend a few minutes researching the day's Wonderopolis question—or other curiosities they have in their notebook (left over from the article of the week, the class wonder wall, or the everyday curriculum).

One day, the Wonderpolis question was "How are holograms made?" The students were fascinated when they started to research. They couldn't believe that holograms are not just in Star Wars, but found on money, credit cards, and even on chocolate candy wrappers. One student discovered that in some Russian parking lots, a hologram of a person in a wheelchair appears if you try to park in a handicapped space illegally! Shortly before the end of the inquiry time, students briefly share or go public, either at their tables or in a larger group.

Thursday: On "Throwback Thursdays," Julie projects one or more historical photos on the class Padlet. This app works like an online sheet of paper on which you can place content (e.g., images, text, videos, documents) anywhere on the page; then around the edges, individual kids can digitally post their thinking. The last time I was in her class on a Thursday, Julie projected the image of an historic battlefield in a tropical climate, along with a couple of mysterious flags. After the kids and I struggled with the clues for ten minutes, student José, who had been wearing an ill-concealed grin throughout, told us all that this was the Battle of Puebla, the triumph that ended the Mexican War of Independence. Julie had chosen this battle scene because today was, ta-da, Cinco de Mayo!

During "Throwback Thursdays," students work in groups of four or five, scattered around the classroom. They "talk" to each other through Padlet by typing in ideas, asking questions, responding, and posting theories. (Though pictures can be projected on a regular screen and kids' conversations can also happen on paper, the digital version seems especially engaging.) When students have an inkling of the photo's meaning, they can open another tab to research their ideas. Finally, kids post links to other photos, articles, and websites to help their team determine what the mystery photo is all about.

Notice how each day's soft start has a strong structure combined with an inherently interesting topic, so kids start every day actively learning, while keeping focused and on track.

POINT OUT

Friday: As the week winds down, the final soft start is "Fuel for Thought Fridays." Julie explains how it works: "One of my favorite books, *365 Days of Wonder* by R. J. Palacio, is filled with pithy and thought-provoking sayings by famous people. The book sits out in my room and kids come by and flag quotes they want to explore. When I approve one of their choices, they eagerly scribe it on our easel pad on a Friday for us all to ponder."

Students first read the quote on their own, jotting responses in their notebooks. Next, they gather on the carpet with a partner. Every pair reads the quote aloud, and after some conversation, they gather back as a whole to share and discuss. Sometimes, there's a quick whip around to listen to everyone's ideas and build on each other's thinking.

A recent quote was: "We love the things we love for what they are," by Robert Frost. Pretty heady stuff! Here's what some kids thought about that line:

Piper: "I think the quote means that we should love things for the way they are and not take them for granted."

Christian: "We love things because they are unique."

Lydia: "You accept who people are and not what they have."

Figure 4.4 Glenwood third graders Anlise, Anais, and Brandon enjoy their daily soft starts.

Julie reflects: "Our 'Fuel for Thought Fridays' have really helped the kids to rise above literal thinking. Even though they are working with just ten or twelve artistically chosen words, they are for sure grappling with 'complex text'—and the activity is quick, collaborative, and fun. So often, when we finish discussing a quotation, someone will blurt out: 'Wow! How do people think like that? That's deep!'"

GIVE STUDENTS A RANGE OF SOFT START CHOICES
Find your own way into the day

Faith Shellabarger, Katie Block, Abby Schmitz, and **Ashley Ohmstede,** fifth-grade teachers at Eason Elementary School

The soft start in Eason's fifth-grade rooms takes place immediately after their rockin' fifteen-minute dance party. Yes, you heard that correctly; if you missed the description, go back to Chapter 2, "Develop a Morning Greeting Ritual." The dancing officially ends when the school announcements begin on the intercom, followed by the Pledge of Allegiance (this also serves as a cool-down for the kids). The following soft start is just as quiet and focused as the dance part was loud and meandering. It is open-ended and always driven by student choice. Kids find a special place in the room to get comfortable and dive in; the norm is quiet, individual work. Here are some of the choices offered by teachers Katie, Faith, Ashley, and Abby.

1. Read independently
Sit, lounge, or cluster together and read. Students have a mix of independently chosen fiction and nonfiction books in the classroom library, as well as two

book-club books each. They can also read magazines, newspapers, or websites. To feed each other reading tips and generate fresh reading choices, they can post to a Padlet or a wall chart called "What are you reading?" Often several kids will pull right up close, so that they are almost touching each other, but still read or write silently (see Figure 4.5).

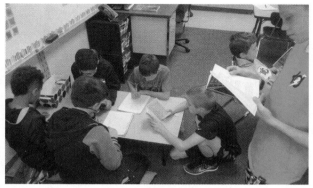

Figure 4.5 Boys working during soft start. No talking here.

2. Free write

Students are allowed to write in any form in their notebooks, on computers, or on any other surface or device within reach. Faith says that this soft start time has unleashed some unexpected authors in her room, especially among boys. "I have a lot of what I like to call "sneaky writers," kids who tend to be soft-spoken and shy in a group, but give them a notebook and a pen, and oh baby oh! These students are so creative—but they don't succeed when commanded what or how to write. Our soft start gives them time to pursue writing in their own way."

3. Scan the headlines

Faith shares another option: "There are some students who love to come in the morning and find out what's going on in the world. They will look up the most recent sports stats for their favorite teams; get on the *Today* show website and see any news updates or feature stories; watch videos on CNN; check the class Twitter feed to see some of the updates from entities or groups we follow (National Aeronautics and Space Administration, National Geographic, Wonderopolis, Popular Science, the History Channel), or check kid news sites like Newsela, DOGO News, or TIME for Kids."

4. Passion projects

Ashley Ohmstede pioneered the fourth soft start choice—passion time, aka free inquiry. She let her kids kick off their shoes, grab a notebook, and do personal inquiry into any area that interested them, as long as it was purposeful and educational. She modeled for kids how, in her own free time, she looked up new recipes or gardening ideas on Pinterest. Then she invited kids to list some of their own interests, and they were off and running.

From across the hall, Katie adds: "We tried this passion time in my class using the same format that Ashley had created, and it was wonderful! We decided this would be incorporated into our morning routine from then on. The kids were so engaged and didn't want the time to end. (Who ever does want their free learning time to end, though?) My students created what we call their Innovate! notebook, which serves as a catchall for all their passion time curiosities, ongoing inquiry findings, and designs for inventions and ambitious moon shots."

POINT OUT

The Eason teachers are telling us about five soft start choices they offer kids. In the last model, Julie Eisenhauer mentioned five others. You will probably want to develop some additional soft starts tailored to your own students. These need to be simple and repeatable, so kids can quickly choose one and get to work. To ensure engagement, they need to either evoke or provoke kids' curiosity (definitely not worksheets!). And we want our chosen soft starts to pave the way to further inquiry, whether for individuals, teams, or the whole class.

5. Post to book clubs

Faith explains the last of the soft start choices: "Since these students are in two book clubs at all times (one fiction and one nonfiction), they often get excited to share about a certain part they have just read. They may want to remind themselves to bring up this section during their next book club meeting—or, if they just can't wait, to immediately begin an online chat about an exciting part with other members of their group. So, to create an outlet for this online book chat, we teachers set up the social media platform Edmodo for our kiddos. It works like "Facebook for school," because you can post, like, and comment on your friends' posts.

Each book club has a private feed that only the members of that group can see. So, during their morning soft starts, many kids chose to post possible discussion topics for their next face-to-face book club meetings."

The Eason crew normally gives about fifteen minutes for kids to range among these choices. With the dance party happening beforehand, kids have a half hour every morning when they can socialize, deepen friendships, blow off some steam, activate their curiosity, and do some self-directed reading or investigating. As Faith says: "Our soft start just eases us right into our morning. Students are always so respectful and productive after they've had a chance to choose their own path into the day. And we teachers love it too, since we have time to get our ducks in a row—and finish that morning cup of coffee as kids do their chosen work."

Our urge to start the school day with a prompt, teacher-directed, whole-class activity probably got implanted in our DNA during our own years at school (and was certainly reinforced in college). A top-of-the-morning roundup is practically a defining feature of a teacher-centered classroom; right after the flag salute, the commander stands up and gives marching orders to the troops.

But in school, we have other choices, even if we haven't exercised them very often. We can create opening structures, norms, and patterns that allow a gentle, thoughtful, personalized entry into the flow of learning. Soft starts are an investment in the rest of the day. If kids begin the morning by exercising their own curiosity, under their own control, they are more likely to be engaged and curious all day long.

Looked at over a whole day of school, a fifteen-minute soft start is an investment in the overall seven-hour outcome. Kids will accomplish more "net learning" if they start that day in the driver's seat.

5

Check Our News Feed

why

Among the strongest sparks for kids' inquiry projects are current news items. We find these in kid-appropriate newspapers, magazines, media, and online sources.

"Let's see what's in the news today. Maybe we will find something we want to know more about. It could be about one of the topics we are already studying or something completely new."

what

We Might Say to Kids

how

Checking over today's news events can be a five- or fifteen-minute job. If kids pick a topic to investigate, as individuals or as a class, that can take another fifteen minutes—or another few class sessions.

Long It Might Take

When I began teaching sixth graders in Santa Fe, I inherited a wonderful asset—a classroom subscription to the *Santa Fe New Mexican*, a small-town daily with a decent selection of national and international coverage. Following the example of my colleague Joyce Sanchez, I began the morning with all of us simply reading the paper. The norm arose that you could point out a story to a friend quietly, but that for the first five or seven minutes, mostly all we heard was the sound of pages turning. On any given day, kids might be reading about war in the Middle East, about athletic doping scandals, or about how scientists now think that a unicorn-like creature really did live with early humans (this was the unlovely, pre-Disneyized version, but it did have a single horn).

Then we'd shift into discussion. A kid would "nominate" an article for us all to chew on for a while. If we hadn't read that story already, we'd flip back and skim it. Then the student would tell what struck her about it, and the conversation was on. When that petered out, we'd shift to another story some student had flagged; typically we would get to two or three each time.

After a few minutes, we'd decide what to do next. Some days, we'd just move along to our next order of business—the reading and conversation were enough. Other times, I'd choose one article to put under the document camera and read a couple paragraphs aloud, stopping to model how I inferred, or connected, or analyzed the text. And quite often, we'd find a story that was so fascinating we just had to learn more. Like the day when scores of dangerous animals escaped from some goofball's private (and illegal) zoo in Ohio. When these urgently interesting topics came up, we followed the same steps you'll hear from the four news-feed models in this chapter. We divided up into teams and investigated our favorite stories, right on the spot. (See two boys doing just that in Figure 5.1.)

Figure 5.1 Jack and David report on the return of U.S. astronaut Scott Kelly.

Try This

We probably don't think of ourselves as persons with an official "news-feed." We just gather the news casually, seemingly incidentally, as we go through the day, right? But if we look more closely at our habits, we may be more systematic than we thought.

Here's the experiment: jot down every news source you consult during a normal weekday. When I did this myself, I realized how many sources I use regularly—and I noticed some categories that might help you make your own inventory. Remember, my sources are not recommendations—your list might be entirely different. I also confess that, because of my job as an author and consultant, I may gobble more media than other teachers.

Magazines

I read old-fashioned paper magazines every morning, two cups of coffee worth.

Books

I read professional books for educational news and developments.

Popular nonfiction books (e.g., *Tribe* by John Krakauer) hook me like novels.

TV

My wife and I watch the national news nightly, as well as *60 Minutes* and other shows with news content.

We also watch cable news, but are trying to cut down.

Radio

While driving around, we listen to NPR and various SiriusXM channels.

Web

My daily news briefs are from Educational Leadership, National Council of Teachers of English, and *Education Week*.

I subscribe to the *New York Times, Santa Fe New Mexican*, and *Washington Post*.

Web Apps/Sites

With the help of my phone or my laptop, I read:

- Email, through which various news bulletins come in daily
- Twitter, where people I follow post great articles and I try to reciprocate
- Facebook, to find news about my own children
- Wonderopolis, a favorite curiosity-feeding site for kids— and for me

Look at your own listing and see what your own favorite news sources are. Think about which ones you could use with, or adapt for, your students. And give a look at the several news-for-kids resources that appear in this chapter.

When we regularly put kids in touch with news sources, we want to be sure that information is age-appropriate and isn't shocking, worrisome, or overwhelming to children. Luckily, we live in a time when carefully curated books and web resources for young people abound. We can trust *National Geographic*, Time for Kids, and Newsela for both accurate and appropriate information. In Chapter 9, we'll consider how inquiry can help us when upsetting news does penetrate our classrooms, which unavoidably happens during every school year.

Today we have web tools like Symbaloo, where you can put links to all kids' favorite news sources on one page, creating a personalized modern-day news ticker (see Figure 5.2). Fifth-grade teacher Katie Block explains how she uses it: "Symbaloo is really just a place to keep bookmarks that you and your kids can access from any device. I started by going to Symbaloo.com and creating an account (just with my email address). In the settings, you can make it public and share the link. I've bookmarked this as the homepage for our classroom devices and have posted the link on our class blog for students to access from anywhere."

Figure 5.2
Symblaloo page for Katie Block's fifth graders as of mid-September

To keep it gradual, Katie models clicking just one link a day—which means checking out a single resource each day, like Time for Kids or Newsela. She models how to access the site, log in (if needed), and locate articles. Then she gives students an opportunity to explore the resource individually or with a partner.

Over the first month of school, students learn how the many different kid news sites work. By mid-September this year, Katie's kids were using *Tween Tribune*, Wonderopolis, *TIME for Kids*, PBS Learning Media, Kids Discover, KidRex, Newsela, DOGO News, The Kid Should See This, *Sports Illustrated Kids*, Around the World, Teaching Kids News, AEA Online, Today's Meet, Multiple Intelligences, *Everyday Math*, Khan Academy, Photos of Class, Edmodo, SeeSaw, KidBlog, Piktochart, Venngage, Smore, and a few other customized links.

Another way to begin (or an option to switch to after kids have some experience) is to invite your kids to review the dozens of available news sources for students, pick their own favorites, and create a "tile" for each one. Then, using their customized Symbaloo page, they can quickly check what's happening in newsrooms, countries, museums, research centers, and webcams all around the world.

SET UP A NEWS TICKER
Reading the headlines

Laura Olson, fifth-grade teacher at Eason Elementary School

Every Thursday morning, my students take twenty to thirty minutes for independent nonfiction reading, which mainly means checking out the news. They get on our iPads or laptops and explore Newsela, Wonderopolis, PBS Kids, Kids Discover, *Smithsonian*, Scholastic, and local newspaper articles online. Sometimes they can choose any resource or topics they're curious about. Other times, with curricular topics in mind, I'll direct them to one or two resources or give them specific topics to investigate.

Whatever the subject, this is mostly independent work, but I do set two parameters:

- Stick to school-appropriate topics like science, current events, kids, art, money, sports, and health.

- If you are using Newsela, choose the right reading level for you. (This online news resource allows the user to choose between five different lexile levels). Reminding students about reading level signals my struggling readers to choose a manageable level of challenge, and not get bogged down attempting the adult-level version that's always the initial choice.

This past couple of months, my kids have tackled:

- Natural disasters—sinkholes, earthquakes, volcanoes, tsunamis

- Migration—European immigrants to America, Ellis Island, Angel Island, orphan trains

- U.S. Civil War—battlefields, important people, weapons

- Physical and cultural features of a region—deserts, rain forests, mountains, language, religion, foods

- Inventions and innovations—pet cameras, basketball

The kids take notes in their content notebooks or just on a sticky (more informally) and then we usually share our new learning or any lingering questions during our morning meeting.

I encourage them to talk with peers while they're exploring, so there are lots of conversations during this time. Addison and Emma were exploring information about Abraham Lincoln and they went back and forth sharing new learning and facts about his life. Jojo, Timmy, Seth, and Brendan were all surprised to learn that Abraham Lincoln didn't really like to be called Abraham or Abe, but preferred to go by Lincoln. Brenna, Norah, and Hazim were watching a video on landslides and talked about how weird it was to watch a mountain split in half. Then we had a sinkhole that opened up right in Des Moines! To learn more, we looked at the *Des Moines Register*'s report online. Brendan and Seth were wondering if there had been any pipes in the house and if those would have been sucked down in the ground too.

On a free-choice day, Sophie summarized an article about a man who was farming bugs to eat them! Of course, her classmates squealed with disgust and laughed when she shared this. We were all curious about this topic, and Sophie went on to explain that insects are actually eaten in many countries, sometimes in soups or crisp-fried. She also reported that babies are fed bugs because they're high in iron, which helps prevents anemia. The kids loved all this fascinating-yucky info, but I was also able to connect Sophie's findings to our curriculum about the cultural features of different regions, and how foods are an important aspect of all cultures.

POINT OUT

Here's a theme that gets stronger for me with every school I visit. When in doubt, *ask the kids.* What shall we read next, how long should we spend on this, how do we solve this problem? And especially: How did it go?

When I asked the kids what they enjoyed about following the news, they had plenty to say:

Bella: I liked that we could search what we wanted. I like to learn new things. I learned about sleep walking.

Ansley: We got to use technology. Girls are getting injuries in gymnastics. Sports. Wonders of the day for summer.

Madeline: I liked Newsela so I can type in a question and get answers. Why is glitter sparkly? How is the sun hot when it is in space and space is cold?

Jojo: Learned more about the world and the past. Brands of tennis shoes sales. How did LeBron James get a shoe endorsement when he was in high school?

Emma: Research for what you didn't know. What is a *ghost town*?

Hazim: When we did petcube cam. You could watch your pet from far away to make sure they are safe. Read latest news or new inventions.

Addison: It was fun to read different articles. Sea World not breeding orcas. I don't usually do research at home.

Colin: Fun to learn new stuff. First emperor of China. What is the biggest diamond in the world?

Alexis: Learn new stuff ahead of time. No Russian woman has won a figure skating competition. What is the coolest gem in the world?

Norah: Easy to come in and relax and look at it. Birds that were making slides out of the sand. Can animals know what you are saying?

Cooper: I liked on Wonderopolis how you could watch a video and read so I could understand more. Does heat affect how high a ball bounces? When will football end or will it end?

My curious kids love to follow the news, especially when they have a chance to explore the most interesting headlines for themselves. I hope this will get them in the habit of being critical readers and, when they are adults, alert citizens who actively ponder and study the news.

FOLLOW A WEBCAM

Our year of eagles

Beth Kaminski, first-grade teacher at Glenwood School

Since January, Beth Kaminski's first graders have had the privilege of observing the life of an eagle family every day. Nested in a tall tree in rural Georgia, this majestic nuclear family—Mother, Father, and two quickly growing eaglets—has been available for twenty-four-hour viewing via three webcams mounted right in the tree (see one frame in Figure 5.3). Now it is May, and the eaglets, which the kids watched hatch and grow, are getting ready to fly! Hats off to

Figure 5.3 Freeze frame from Berry College eagle cam
Reprinted with express permission of Berry College, Inc.

Berry College for making this awesome resource (www.berry.edu/eaglecam) available to kids (and grown-ups) around the country.

The eagle family became an integral part of Ms. K's classroom—sometimes its main focus, and sometimes in the background. Beth explains:

> When students come to school in the morning, the nest cam is already projected on my smartboard. Kids follow their regular morning routine: unpacking their backpacks, signing up for lunch, getting their book bins, and so on. When the kids are ready, they stop by the screen and 'check-in' with the birds. Whatever they notice happening, especially new developments, they write about it in their observation journals.
>
> In addition to recording in their observation journals, kids created a timeline poster chronicling the main events. [See p. xi.] This began in early January when kids noticed activity at the nest site. Mom and Dad eagle were adding fresh branches to their already existing nest. We learned from the Berry College website that eagles will not take branches they find on the ground, but instead gnaw fresh branches off a tree! We even got to see Mom eagle carrying a pretty big branch in her one talon. We were disappointed when she dropped it right before she made it back to the nest. Of course the real fun began in February when we noticed the first egg and then the next day, egg number two! Later, we added to the timeline when we first saw Dad bring a fish to the nest for Mom. And finally the moment we were all waiting for—we saw the pip in the eggs [the beginning of the eaglet breaking out of the shell].

After the first few morning viewings, Beth decided to leave the webcam on all day. She explains to curious classroom visitors:

> The drama of the eagle family's life is unfolding before us, and the opportunity to witness it "live" and up close is such authentic, joyful learning. Why would we turn it off?

Predictably, people also wonder if the eagle vigil ever became a distraction, or interrupted other work. Sure, Beth says:

> There are moments during writing or reading workshop when someone notices Mom or Dad delivering a fish and feeding it to the young ones, beak to beak. Who can ignore that? The kids all drop what they are currently doing, grab their observation journals, and record what they see! We

can easily return to our previous tasks with plenty of smiles and with our curiosity energized.

Beth's intentional decision to *invite interruptions* into her class day is an unusual move, and not for everyone. But the eagle quest didn't begin until January, when she felt her kids were capable of shifting between topics while maintaining their focus.

POINT OUT

One day Beth was reading a story to the kids on the rug in front of the smartboard. As she was reading aloud, one student noticed that both eaglets were sitting nicely together on the edge of the nest, on the side facing the class, and it looked like they were attentively enjoying the story. The kids inferred that the eaglets must love books. Beth reports:

That's when the students got the idea to change one of our reading corners into an eagles' habitat. Some kids turned our donated papasan chair (a wicker base with a wicker bowl seat) into a nest, making branches out of rolled brown paper. Another group of kids painted a forest background, while others made an eagle and two eaglets for the nest out of rolled-up paper "sticks." [See their handiwork in Figure 5.4.] Everybody worked on making labels and writing facts about the eagles. Finally a big comfy blanket was put on the basket and this became the kids' favorite reading spot!

Figure 5.4 Full-size eagles' nest constructed in Beth's classroom

Visitors often asked Beth if the first graders had named "their" eaglets. She replied:

No, we did not name them, but we sure did discuss it in depth. We learned from experts that it's best not to name baby animals, because they are wild and we shouldn't get too attached. (Of course, it was too late for that!) Another eagle cam in Colorado had a big spring snowstorm in mid-April. All three eaglets in that nest perished. We learned a hard fact of nature that day: 40 percent of fledglings do not survive their first year—and we have kept our fingers crossed since then.

The Berry College webcam also featured a periodic live chat with a bird biologist, so the kids eagerly submitted questions for that event:

- How long will the fledgings practice flying before they leave the nest for good?

- Why do some eaglets not survive leaving the nest?

- What happens? Do Mom and Dad eagle teach the eaglets how to hunt for food?

- Will the new eagles stay in the area after they learn to fly or will they fly somewhere new?

- When will their head feathers turn white?

Later, they tuned into the live chat with Berry College professor Renee Carlton. Beth said the kids were a little disappointed when their school's name wasn't mentioned, but "some other kids asked the same questions we did—and we gobbled up the answers!"

> For some time, the kids were wondering why the nest always looked so clean—meaning, where did the eaglets "use the bathroom"? A few days later, we had the privilege of witnessing an eaglet on the very edge of the nest but facing in with its back tail hanging over the edge. It was with total fascination (remember—we are six) when we realized the bird was "using the bathroom"! Just yesterday, when we were busy writing, someone in class noticed this behavior happening again in the nest and yelled out, "Bombs away!"

There were many unplanned eagle activities that the kids themselves initiated. After spending one morning poring over mentor texts to discover how authors bring characters to life, the kids decided to use their newfound knowledge of writing dialogue during that rainy day's indoor recess. Beth came into the room to find the kids sitting in front of the screen drawing pictures of the two unattended young eagles in the nest. As she unobtrusively observed, they inserted speech bubbles in their pictures (writing what they imagined the eagles would be saying to each other). (See Figure 5.5.) Beth recalls, "I arrived just in time to hear Sophia say, 'Hey, observing this eagles' nest every day is just like looking at a wordless picture book. It's telling us a story!'

In their fifth month of observation, Beth knew that the birds' "childhood" would culminate soon. As the eaglets were getting ready to fledge, they noticed a lot of wing flapping and hopping around the nest. Then there was "branching," where they would hop-fly to nearby branches.

Figure 5.5 Kids storyboarding eagle family dialogue

Even though my kids had grown to dearly love these honorary members of our classroom, they were really looking forward to the eaglets' first flight. To be part of this celebration, we researched how to make paper airplanes, which kids modified with marbles, markers, and plastic spoons to look like eagles. Then, on April 26, the nest suddenly emptied as our adopted Georgia eagles took off on their maiden flights! We ran outside and celebrated by launching our own paper eagles into the bright Wisconsin sky! [See Figure 5.6]

Figure 5.6 First graders celebrate "fledging day" by launching their own handmade eagles.

```
FROM: Beth Kaminski
TO: Harvey Daniels
RE: Will this madness ever end?

Hey Smokey, right before we were leaving to go home this
afternoon we saw a photograph on the Berry College site
of an eagle feather found on the ground by the nest. It's
```

12 inches long and 4 inches wide. Found out that bald eagles have 7,000 feathers. Also found out that it is illegal to take an eagle's feather—possibly even to pick one up. I could barely get the kids out the door. "How can it be against the law to take an eagle feather on the ground?" "When the feather falls to the ground who does it belong to now?" "Why?" "Why?" "Why?" I promised the kids that we will explore all this first thing tomorrow, as I'm literally trying to get them out the door so they don't miss their buses!! Thank you, eagles, for keeping us curious!!!!!

PS: Today we found a new webcam with the cutest baby owls!

Webcams for Kids

There are loads of webcams around the world today, and many of them are guaranteed curiosity-sparkers. You don't need to stick with the same one for five months, like Beth's eagle watchers did. Short visits are great too. Here are some interesting choices:

San Diego Zoo: animal cams and videos of pandas, polar bears, apes, elephants

Earth Cams for Kids: chicken run cam, chicken coop cam, Merlin the Talking Parrot

Smithsonian National Zoo: elephants, pandas (Mei Xiang and Bei Bei), and lion cubs

Alaska Department of Fish and Game: web and trail cams; walrus, bear, salmon, loons

Animal Planet: coral reef with audio, cockroach cam!

Animal webcams are certainly big favorites of kids (and adults), but there are plenty of webcams focused on other interesting subjects. SkylineWebcams.com provides views of:

International cities: Rome, Prague, Rio, London, Times Square in New York

World heritage sites: Pyramids of Giza; Western Wall, Jerusalem; Imam Riza Holy Shrine in Iran; the Coliseum in Rome; Grand Canal, Venice

Natural wonders: Norwegian fjord

Oddities: Doggie Day Care; Delaware Department of Motor Vehicles waiting room—"Have a seat, this might take a while."

LET KIDS GATHER THE NEWS

Meet Inky the Octopus

Beth Kaminski, first-grade teacher; **Megan Dixon**, second-grade teacher; and **Sarah Van Lieshout**, third-grade teacher at Glenwood School

One of the kids' favorite news stories last year was the escape of an octopus from captivity in New Zealand. According to news reports at the time, Inky, who had been captured from a nearby reef and held in a laboratory for several years, took advantage of a lapse in overnight security to make his exit. Aquarium manager Rob Yarrall explained that "the lid to the octopus' tank was left slightly ajar after maintenance one night. Inky found this rather tempting, and climbed out. He managed to make his way to one of the drain holes that go back to the ocean, and off he went—didn't even leave us a message, just off and went!" (Beeler 2016). As you may have experienced firsthand, kids around the world went wild with this feel-good story, as postings like "Run Inky Run!" and "Houdini Octopus Fools His Keepers" popped up all over the Internet.

At Glenwood School, the first and second graders were no less excited. They naturally wanted to study octopi—or octopuses—right now. Beth Kaminski, Megan Dixon, and coach Deb Zaffiro gathered resources from around the school (luckily, there were a few books about octopi and related critters in the bookroom and library). And since the media was going nuts on this story, they found plenty of kid-friendly articles they could bookmark or print.

Beth tells what happened in her room:

> The kids were so excited I decided to do a whole-group "Octopus Ink-quiry." Our coach Deb Zaffiro started the ball rolling by sending us a link to the Inky news before school even started. So we began our day by reading an article (projected on the smartboard) about Inky, the great escape artist. The kids were totally hooked! As the day went on, we kept coming back to Inky. The kids found books and articles during their independent reading time. We made an octopus on a bulletin board and the kids posted their questions about Inky and Houdini—the great human escape artist—and we even researched and generated a list of plural words that do not end in *s*!
>
> The next morning we started our day by discussing some questions we had come up with the day before. Bella wondered if we had an octopus at our own zoo. Many of the kids said yes, because they had seen it. So of course we were very interested in finding out about our own local specimen. We immediately emailed the Milwaukee County Zoo and discovered that it is home to a giant Pacific octopus named Kayin, which means "the long-awaited child." We learned that Kayin likes to hide in her den by moving the rocks around and building a fort. She can change her body shape and color to look like the rocks. When she wants people to see her she can change her texture and skin color back again.
>
> In our research we learned about how truly intelligent octopi are and about their numerous escapes from captivity. As a result we felt it was our duty as "octopus experts" to inform the zoo of this fact! Most of us were very relieved to find out that, yes, the zoo was well aware of this risk and puts an acrylic top on the aquarium instead of a movable mesh top. We ended this whole-group inquiry after two days by writing a shared fun-fiction story about Kayin's escape from the Milwaukee County Zoo. Even though our

whole-group inquiry ended, many of the kids began writing their own stories about Kayin's escape, which had her basking at Bradford Beach on Lake Michigan! Others wrote newspaper articles for our news board, and still others worked on designing ways to keep an octopus from escaping from its tank.

Upstairs in second grade, Megan read aloud "Inky the Octopus Escapes from New Zealand Aquarium" from the *New York Times* (so much for reading levels). The kids immediately came up with their own octopus questions.

- Is it OK to cage an octopus if it's smart enough to get out?

- Have other sea animals escaped in captivity?

- What makes an octopus' body able to escape through such a small hole?

Some kids investigated how Inky, weighing fifty pounds, could get through the small drain hole on the lab floor. They found out that octopuses can squeeze through an opening as small as their own mouths (properly called *beaks*, which are the only hard part of their body.) The rest of an octopus, as we know, is pretty mushy and flexible. The kids still wondered—wouldn't Inky have been cut or scraped while sliding down that long, rough pipe to the ocean? Probably not, they discovered, because that slime on an octopus' body would lubricate him and prevent injuries along his escape route.

Across the hall in Sarah's third-grade classroom, the Inky Project unfolded similarly—even though a substitute teacher was on duty the day of the inquiry. After some planning with her colleagues, Sarah simply left a few guidelines for the sub, and the inquiry was a success. What this shows is (1) they have great subs at Glenwood and (2) when kids have done a lot of inquiry, they can manage themselves!

The more kids learned about this animal, the better they could understand and appreciate its escape. They found out that octopi are naturally curious and exceptionally smart, even though they are close cousins of snails (a fact noted on the poster in Figure 5.7). In fact, they are notorious among scientists for escaping from aquariums; Inky was far from the first octopus to plot a breakout.

After reading about caging octopi, another group wanted to design the ideal habitat for a captive octopus. They made a poster of this dream

Figure 5.7 Inky poster notes that "octopus cuzin is a snail."

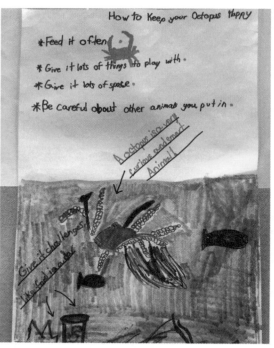

Figure 5.8 Octopus care poster: The final product of a newsfeed inquiry

environment, "How to Keep Your Octopus Happy" (see Figure 5.8), with reminders that specified:

- Feed it often
- Give it lots of stimuli
- Give it lots of space
- Be careful about other animals you put in
- Give it a challenge like food in a jar

Kids love the news. After all, what could compete with the amazing, glorious, crazy, peculiar, and suspicious things people and animals and unicorns are up to every day? As the old expression goes: You can't make this stuff up! The teachers in this chapter have shown us many ways to welcome kid-hooking news items into the day, while screening out upsetting or inappropriate stories. Not only can the news stimulate inquiry projects of all sorts, it also sets children on a path to becoming active, aware, and critical citizens of their communities and of the world.

6

Hang Out with an Expert

why

Teachers try as hard as they can to be knowledgeable in many fields. But kids also need exposure to real-life experts, people who have spent their whole lives developing knowledge in a single field, craft, or profession. So in inquiry projects, we try to connect kids with adult specialists in the field. By getting face time with experts, students learn authentic and reliable information, and also witness what passionate and sustained devotion to a specialty looks like.

what

"We have been studying the ecology of our local watershed for a week now. We've done a lot of reading, looked at some videos, searched the web for maps and information, and learned some key vocabulary. I think now would be a good time to learn more from a real expert in the field, someone who works on our environment every day. So next Tuesday. . . ."

We Might Say to Kids

how

Fifteen to twenty minutes for a short recorded or live video visit; an hour or more for a flesh-and-blood expert working with your class, at school or in the community.

Long It Might Take

My sixth graders in Santa Fe always loved it when we reached out to experts beyond our classroom (perhaps because it meant a break from *me*). When some of my students got interested in animal rights, we emailed Mark Beckoff, a renowned biology professor at the University of Colorado and author of an awesome book called *The Emotional Lives of Animals* (2007). We were all delighted when he wrote back promptly, offering a telephone conference call from his home in the Rocky Mountains. On the appointed day, we crowded into the conference room, where our school's only speakerphone lived. Dr. Beckoff talked for over an hour about animals' feelings, and answered every kid's question. The only interruption came when he suddenly shushed us. "There's a red fox walking across my deck right now," he whispered, and we could almost see it leaving tracks in the February snow.

When another group of my kids started researching nuclear weapons, all I had to do was call Los Alamos National Laboratory, only thirty miles from Salazar School, and order up a nuclear physicist! Yes, our school is just down the road from where the nuclear bombs used in World War II were made—and every warhead in America's arsenal returns regularly to be "refurbished." The gracious Dr. Robert Eisenstein appeared a few days later to answer a long list of questions prepared by a roomful of respectful and fascinated kids. A couple of boys I've written about earlier (Harvey and Daniels 2015) took Dr. Eisenstein's explanation of the rationale for Hiroshima and made it a multiweek quest for understanding.

So here's one takeaway about using experts to evoke students' interest and enhance their inquiries: adults, even highly recognized and busy professionals, have a soft spot in their hearts for kids and for helping out teachers. If someone asked them to do any other chore, they'd say, "Sorry, no way, I am just too swamped right now." But if some nine-year-olds want to learn about their profession? They'll take half a day off to come to your school.

The more you seek out experts, the more opportunities you'll find for working with them—and you can collaborate with teachers around the building to find the experts you need. Over the years, Duke School has developed a robust file of experts—parents, community members, employees at local companies and nonprofits, professors from nearby universities—who are great at teaching kids, and

Try This

Think back on your own most memorable days in elementary school. Take all the time you need—this is a lot harder for some of us than others! Now, what made those red-letter days stand out and last in your mind? Based on my conversations with thousands of former students, the days we remember most are those when we went out on a field trip—or had an outside expert come in.

For example, when I was in fifth grade, we went to the Skippy peanut butter factory—I remember every second of that narrated visit, along with the yummy PB&J sandwich they gave us at the end of the tour—with a carton of milk! The "master cooker" answered all of our questions, but later I found myself wondering, why did they have to pour those huge barrels of oil in with the peanuts? Now, part of the thrill factor for those days might have been the change of pace, but we can recollect how our curiosity was sparked as well.

What field trips or expert visits can you recall? What ways have you found to put experts in front of your students?

who love to make themselves available. For Duke students, it's normal to see ten experts a year, either on campus or at the expert's workplace, bakery, or farm.

To children, the greatest experts of all are their beloved picture book and chapter book authors: people like Kevin Henkes, Seymour Simon, Christopher Paul Curtis, and Patricia Polacco definitely have celebrity status among our young ones, and meeting personally with one of them is spectacular when it can happen. But authors like these have lots of fans, can only travel so much, and have other books to write! So we can sometimes arrange live video visits, which some authors offer via Skype or FaceTime, usually for a fee. Other authors have posted online videos of themselves answering kids' most common questions about books, characters, and their personal writing habits.

Sources of Author Interviews

- Reading Rockets has a huge collection of recorded interviews from A-list authors like Eve Bunting, Eric Carle, Jon Scieszka, Chris Van Allsburg, and Patricia Polacco. www.readingrockets.org/books/interviews

- The website NBC Learn has a feature called Writers Speak to Kids, with interviews from Jacqueline Woodson, Mo Willems, Gordon Korman, and others. www.nbclearn.com/writers-speak-to-kids

- ChildrensBooks.about.com offers "10 Videos About Favorite Children's Authors and Illustrators." (These are life stories, not interviews.) Maurice Sendak, Dr. Seuss, Jerry Pinkney, Roald Dahl, Beverly Cleary, and others are featured.

- YouTube is a surprising resource. Search any of your kids' favorite authors on YouTube, and you're likely to find several interviews, as well as publisher promotions and read-alouds of varying quality recorded by fans and wannabes. You have to be selective about which items are valuable for kids, but there's gold to be found. A recent search on Kevin Henkes, one of my most beloved writers, yielded *seven pages* of mostly excellent videos about him and his work.

You'll never know for sure where connecting with an expert may lead. Beth Kaminski and her first graders sought a relationship with author Tedd Arnold of "Fly Guy" fame. As savvy connoisseurs of Arnold's series, Beth's kids brainstormed a clever new book idea for him, designed a mockup of the cover, and mailed it off. After a months-long interval, back came an email from Ted saying he was taking the kids' suggestion and dedicating the book to them, each by name! As part of his thank-you, he scheduled a school visit with them when *The Fly Guy Presents the White House* came out.

Here come three models for connecting with an expert by hosting a live visitor, meeting on a digital hangout, and building an ongoing relationship, beginning with simple e-mail exchanges. Let's see where these alternatives can lead.

BOOK A PERSONAL APPEARANCE
What's the forecast?

Jessica Lenz, first-grade teacher at Glenwood School

A classic unplanned inquiry happened in Jessica Lenz's first grade when she did a read-aloud of *Super Storms* by Seymour Simon. The kids were immediately hooked on hurricanes, tsunamis, tornadoes, and blizzards (a favorite there in Wisconsin), and wanted to learn more. Jessica made some time for kids to jump into quick research in more books, on their LearnPads, and from web videos. Whatever kind of extreme weather they were investigating, students noticed that the word *meteorologist* came up a lot. They were very curious about what a meteorologist does and how it was related to extreme weather. From what they read, it seemed like a meteorologist would be the perfect person to help answer the many weather questions they still had.

Jessica secretly reached out to a local TV station, Fox 6, and worked it out for Stephanie Barichello (a real live TV meteorologist) to come into the classroom and share her weather wisdom. Jessica continues the story:

> When the confirmation email came, I shared the news with my kids, who were really excited. After savoring the email, we did a Google search of Stephanie Barichello, and watched some video clips of her in action [see Figure 6.1]. Most of the kids recognized her as the woman giving the weather forecast on
>
> TV. They found out that Stephanie had just gotten married and moved to the area from Joliet, Illinois, about a hundred miles away.
>
> The students were thrilled to read a second email from her with details of her upcoming visit. On the appointed morning, kids were ready with a weather graphic organizer where they had listed their lingering questions—those wonders that hadn't been answered in a book or on a website—and that they hoped our expert could answer for us.

Figure 6.1 Meteorologist Stephanie Barichello
Stephanie Barichello, Fox6 News. Used with permission.

Ms. Barichello started her prepared talk, but the first time she paused for questions my kids inundated her with queries from their notes.

Jessica made a "gametime decision" to let kids' questions just surge. She might have forced the kids to be quiet and listen, but with the expert being such a good sport, she decided let her young scientists unleash their enthusiasm and curiosity.

She seemed fine with it and so my first graders sat for an hour just asking her questions like, What makes lightning white? Why do tornadoes mostly touch down in tornado alley? What causes blizzards? Is there such thing as a blizzard alley? What type of storm really is the deadliest? Ms. Barichello didn't even get to share half of the cool tools she had brought along, like a barometer, a PowerPoint of videos and links to superstorms, or her slightly mysterious "tornado in a jar."

The kids were totally engaged, and came away with severe-weather information they'll probably never forget. And the best part: our awesome expert came to us for free. It turns out that most TV stations routinely send their on-air personalities to schools as a public service—and to build loyal viewers from age six up!

HOST A LIVE VIDEO VISIT
Starting a (profitable) theatre company

Amy Lau and **Tery Gunter**, second-grade teachers at Duke School

From pre-K through fifth grade, Duke School has a series of engaging inquiry projects that can be revisited every year. Among these are the Bread Project, Wheels Project, Durham Project, Health Fair Project, River Rangers Project, and Perspectives in Colonial Times Project. For second graders, a favorite spring investigation is the Business Project, during which children create and manage all aspects of a real-life enterprise. This year, Amy Lau's and Tery Gunter's kids decided to form a theatre company. There were plenty of proto-thespians and great singers in this group, so kids were pretty confident about putting on a good performance for the parents and families who would attend. But running the business side wasn't as instinctive. The kids needed some expert guidance on how to make money (or at least break even) in showbiz.

Then a perfect resource appeared. Amy explains, "This particular year we hit the guest expert jackpot. One student's uncle, Michel Hausmann (not to be confused with Michael Haussman, who is a film writer, director, and producer), owns a theatre company, where he also writes, directs, and produces shows. So he knows all aspects of the theatre business. The only drawback is that he lives in Miami and our classroom is in North Carolina! But Mr. Hausmann was too good a resource to pass up, so we decided to try something new—a virtual interview." Once Michel agreed to an online date, Amy and her coteacher, Tery Gunter, did some planning to make sure the remote interview would go off without a hitch. Here's how they ran it, step by step.

To prepare for this event, a number of emails flew back and forth. The teachers explained to Michel what the class was up to and what they hoped he would share. He told them a bit about his theatre, how it operates, what his work life is like—and the teachers passed on this background information to help kids get ready for the visit. Finally, everyone went online to study up on Michel's website and learn more about his theatre business.

Putting all this background information together, the kids brainstormed a list of questions relating to their own work that they hoped Michel could answer. Amy scribed all the key questions on a big chart in black marker, leaving space for the answers on the day of the interview (see Figure 6.2). Finally, Amy emailed a picture

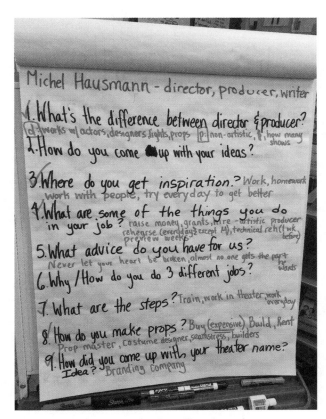

Figure 6.2 Questions for FaceTime interview

with the list of questions to Michel so he would know what to expect the next day, when the conversation went "live."

As with any "video visit," there are plenty of platforms that can do the job—but you need one that works with your classroom's technology. For Amy, the right tool for the job was Apple's FaceTime. So, at the chosen hour, the kids connected with Michel using an iPad mini, projecting him onto the classroom screen using Apple TV. During the interview, the iPad was passed from one child to another. Each student began by introducing her or himself, and then asking a question from the charted list, which was posted near the screen.

As Michel answered their questions, Amy modeled how to jot notes underneath each question (in orange). Once a question was answered, she also checked it off to be sure it wasn't asked again. The kids had been prepped on the importance of asking follow-up or clarifying questions if their initial question was not fully answered.

Amy gives the play-by-play of the big visit:

The interview began the same as any FaceTime interview would, with technical difficulties! The kids were very entertained as we rotated the iPad around and around trying to get everything set up, causing Michel's image on the TV to flip upside down and sideways. It was a great way to break the ice. Once we got our audio and video up and running, the kids were eager to begin. The first person Michel talked to was his own nephew, a quieter student, who politely raised his hand each time before speaking. It was exciting to see this child light up as his uncle appeared on the screen. Michel then asked us what plays we were performing, and the kids proudly shared a brief summary of each one. After getting settled, the tone of the interview was one of seriousness. The students saw this as an opportunity to get some real tips from someone in the theatre business [see Figure 6.3].

One girl was very nervous about an upcoming audition; she had recently suffered a case of stage fright during a school-wide musical performance. She asked Michel what advice he could give to a fellow actor, hoping to find tips and tools to help her get through her audition in front of her teachers and peers. After hearing his response, "Never let your heart be broken," she began to rebuild the confidence she had lost. A number of the students were shocked to hear that Michel still has to practice his acting every day and assigns himself "homework" to stay successful.

Once the interview was over, we debriefed with the children. They looked at my orange notes on our chart and added anything they heard that I missed. We also talked about any advice or themes we took away from our conversation with Michel. The students were excited to learn that being in business involves daily hard work, occasional rejection, teamwork, and the eternal need for money.

Over the next four weeks, the class became consumed with our "Green Globe Dragon Theater." Michel had told us secrets about creating an appeal-

Figure 6.3 Michel, the guest expert, is shown in the large window. One of the second graders can be seen asking a question in the small box in the upper-right-hand corner.

ing business that offers what people want. So, we began by researching what our target audience (parents and other adults in our community) look for in a theatre experience: Do they like comfy seats or hard seats? Do they want funny, silly, or scary costumes? Would they buy coffee, water, or milk? Students designed and distributed a written survey for parents and ran focus groups during Grandparents Day.

Another important insight we took from our hangout with Michel was the many different jobs necessary to run a business. So the children volunteered to work on a committee based on their interests. The marketing committee developed the brand, including a logo and tagline—"Where the Dragon Flies the World." They built a website and designed tickets and posters. The Event Planning Committee drew a floor plan to help the school's maintenance crew understand how they were to set up the chairs and stage. The Finance Committee used the results from our survey and focus groups to make decisions about what we should sell. They researched costs and estimated the budget.

Notice that the expert's advice is still being actively used for weeks after the one-hour meet-up. This shows us the potential benefit of even short conversations with adult experts.

Although we used money from our classroom budget to buy the theatre concessions, we wanted the children to experience borrowing money from an investor. Asking people for loans was one of the big business concerns Michel emphasized during our interview. So after a week of research, the Finance Committee finally presented their request for a loan to our school's Director of Finance and Operations. The loan request was rejected! The students were told they had not given enough information; they needed to collect more and try again. Remembering what Michel had said about "don't let your heart be broken," they came back to the classroom determined to get what was necessary to get Green Globe Dragon Theater the money it needed to commence operations. Their resubmitted budget was approved—whew!

About a month after the Hausmann interview it was showtime. The classroom transformed into our souvenir shop and snack bar, and the common room became the theatre. The children buzzed around with excitement as they sold tickets, snacks, and handmade memorabilia. After shopping, our guests were seated and ready to enjoy the live performance. During the show, the second graders completely transformed into the characters in "Chicken Little" and "Lon Po Po"; all lines were delivered with ease and enthusiasm.

The business was a huge success. There was plenty of money to repay the "loan." The profit was over $400; we decided to split it between Book Harvest (a local organization that donates books to kids who need them) and our school Butterfly Garden. All in all, the students learned the value of teamwork, compromise, and how to thrive in the world of business.

Using Guest Experts in Your Classroom

from Carolynn Klein Hageman, Duke School

Where to find guest experts

- Start with parents.

- Look within your school community.

- Ask professional acquaintances and friends.

- Think about local businesses and organizations.

- Consider government agencies.

- Contact local colleges or universities.

- Be on the lookout when you are in the community.

- Older children can be great experts, too.

- Ask children for their suggestions.

- *Cast a wide net and think outside the box!*

How to coach experts

- Talk with your experts *before* you invite them into your classroom.

- Introduce yourself and talk about the subject matter or project.

- Ascertain their comfort level with the age of students you teach.

- Be very clear what you want the students to gain from the visit.

- Discuss the students' needs and the specifics of the content.

- Describe the teaching space and how much time will be available.

- Take time to answer their questions.

- Offer friendly suggestions.

- See what AV or supplies they night need (paper, Internet connection, etc.).

- Share some of the students' questions with them prior to the visit.

How to coach the children

- Provide students with the background they need to make the most of the visit.

- Brainstorm and list questions prior to the visit.

- Assign roles during the visit; what will each child's job be when the expert comes?

- Go over any note-taking forms or formats you plan to use.

- Ask the children to consider: How will we use the information we will learn to teach our own community?

How to guide the expert visit

- Introduce and restate what the expert will be teaching the children.

- State clearly what the expectations are for the kids during the visit.

- Help keep the expert on track and on time.

- It is OK to redirect or coach the expert.

- Make sure kids get all their prepared questions answered, as well as asking follow-ups during the visit.

- Offer thanks, applause, and gratitude as your expert finishes up.

START WITH AN EMAIL CONVERSATION

History walks through the classroom door

Sara Ahmed, sixth-grade teacher at The Bishop's School and seventh-grade teacher at Burley School

As an elementary and middle school social studies teacher, I have always searched for the ideas that would breathe life into the curriculum. I wanted kids to access history and its big ideas with more excitement than typical textbooks provide. I wanted them to excavate the human stories buried under factual timelines, dates, and battle maps. We need history to come alive in the classroom and show kids connections to the actors from decades and centuries ago; otherwise, it will be just another subject they sit through, day to day.

I kept returning to professional development I received from Facing History and Ourselves, an international organization that provides the tools, strategies, and resources that teachers and students need to do just this. More than anything, FH provided me with a sense of discomfort and the energy of wonder so great that I always left their workshops asking more questions than I came with. Their PD is a dream classroom.

One of the greatest resources that Facing History provides during its programs for teachers is access to witnesses to history. I have heard testimony from Holocaust survivors, refugees, first responders of 9/11, and leaders of the civil rights movement. Dr. Terrence Roberts of the Little Rock Nine was one that has stayed with me for years—mostly because I won't leave him alone, but also because of the way he speaks to, and listens to, kids. [See the young Terrence Roberts in Figure 6.4.]

The first time I heard Dr. Roberts speak, my class was in the middle of reading *Warriors Don't Cry*, a novel by Melba Pattillo Beals, also one of the Little Rock Nine. I was so interested in his message (and I love sharing with the kids when I go to a professional development event), that I had to email him and take a chance on his busy schedule.

Figure 6.4 Little Rock Nine student Terrence Roberts being turned away from Little Rock Central High by Arkansas National Guard in 1957.

© National Park Service/Little Rock Central High National Historic site

From: Sara Ahmed
To: Dr. Terrence Roberts
Sent: Mon, May 16, 2011 3:58:49 PM
Subject: Sara Ahmed from Chicago says thank you!

Hi, Dr. Roberts,

This is Sara Ahmed, one of the Facing History teachers in Chicago Public Schools. It was a pleasure meeting you the other day at our Facing History dinner. Chuck M. always speaks so highly of your relationship with Facing History. I told the kids all about the event, and, of course, they were wowed by how tall you are in the picture and by the time you graciously took with me.

As we discussed at dinner, my students will embark on inquiry projects after we read *Warriors Don't Cry*. Well, one of my students identified you as her number one choice for an investigation. When I asked what she wanted to know about you, she replied, "Everything!"

The class is looking at choices that you and others made at that moment in history. If it is at all possible, would you be willing to answer just a couple questions via email from one of my students? Or, as you'd mentioned, would you pass the questions on to others in the foundation? Whatever you choose is more than appreciated.

Thank you so much. I look forward to hearing from you.

Sara Ahmed

To which he promptly replied, "It would be my pleasure. Yes, I will answer questions and say hello to your students."

I faint.

I tell Maud, who selected Dr. Roberts for her inquiry project. She nearly faints.

She sets out to draft her email in her notebook first. She calls me over to see if her questions are worthy and I give her the green light. Then we quickly gloat about how some of these questions could not be answered if we didn't have the real-life source at our fingertips.

Dr. Roberts,

My name is Maud Grauer, and I'm one of Ms. Ahmed's students. Thank you so much for agreeing to answer some of my questions; this is a huge honor.

- How did your experience at Central High change over time?

- Why did you volunteer to integrate Central?

- Did you encounter any white students that treated you like a human being?

- What were the teachers like?

Once again, thank you.

Maud Grauer

Maud came into class every morning with a coy stare, asking me if he had responded, without actually asking. Three days later, he did.

We both nearly fainted again.

Maud,

In re your questions, I have written my responses below.

- My experience at Central, over time, allowed me to appreciate the opportunity to learn how to control my fear level.

- I volunteered for this experiment in integration because it was the lawful, moral, and necessary thing to do.

- I did in fact encounter some white students who treated me like a human being.

- The teachers, in the main, were unhappy to see us; we represented for them a change too drastic to contemplate.

Dr. Roberts, just as in his speeches, wasted no words in his reply, leaving plenty of room for follow-up questions.

Maud went on to use these answers in her research and create her project, a giant mural of a life-size Dr. Roberts, speaking to his audience through bubbles of text about his experience of integrating Central High. Later that year, when he was in town for another event, Burley had its annual Book Bash, where we celebrate and invite authors to be part of our community. Guess who made a cameo appearance for our middle school kids?

Thanks to Facing History, Dr. Roberts was able to spend time with some eager readers in our classroom, Maud in particular, who couldn't believe that a "character" they read about came to life before their eyes. He sat with the kids on the rug and answered all their questions, even offering some valuable middle school advice about constantly using the words *umm* and *like* when they speak to someone else. (A bonus social skills lesson!)

Later that day, I remember Maud printing out those emails and gingerly gluing them in her notebook. Something totally worth scrapbooking.

A few years later, I moved to San Diego to teach middle school history and I remembered that San Diego was a little closer to Dr. Roberts than Chicago was. *Warriors Don't Cry* was a book club choice in my history class and I paired it with *Lessons from Little Rock,* Dr. Roberts' newly published book, for a few students who wanted further reading.

We can build our list of visiting experts just the way we build our classroom libraries—one by one, patiently, over years. We save their contact information, stay in touch, and never let them go!

POINT OUT

Two of my students, Simran and Jina, jumped at the chance to read it. That was when I mentioned that I knew him and could reach out to him if they had any questions.

"Wait, what?"

I repeated myself.

"Wait. We can like talk to him? Can he come here?" (Lightbulb.)

"Well," I replied with a smile, remembering Dr. Roberts' comments to Maud about speaking, "Only if you promise to not say 'like' a hundred times."

The same way I tried my luck at asking for some email time in Chicago, I did the same in San Diego. This time, however, I could invite Dr. Roberts to visit in person as part of my new school's distinguished speakers series.

From: Sara Ahmed
To: Dr. Terrence Roberts
Sent: Wed, April 17, 2013 9:47:23 AM
Subject: Sara Ahmed, Facing History and Ourselves

Dr. Roberts,

I hope this email finds you well. Last time we met we were in a Roscoe Village café in Chicago, enjoying cornbread and lunch with the Facing History Chicago office. I remember that day well, as you really touched the hearts and minds of my eighth graders at Burley Elementary after we read *Warriors Don't Cry*.

I have since moved to San Diego, and I am teaching in La Jolla at The Bishop's School. I am hoping that we can meet again, this time in California.

My seventh-grade students will be reading *Warriors* and investigating the lives of upstanders during this moment in history. It has been a tremendous journey with them this year, as they came to this with little background knowledge. They are a fantastic bunch of kids.

I don't know what your calendar looks like for the remainder of the academic year. I was just hoping to touch base and see if you are available to be part of this endeavor. It can be a visit, a virtual visit, or whatever suits.

I appreciate your time and hope we can meet on West Coast time very soon!

Best,

Sara Ahmed

After lots of coordination and lots of nudging from my kids who'd read his book, Dr. Roberts was able to join our school community at Bishop's. We made a schedule so kids, teachers, and parents could all have time with him. It brought the community together, and my seventh graders were the Big Men on our 6–12 Campus for at least that day. Jina and Simran introduced Dr. Roberts at an all-school assembly [see Figure 6.5]. In their welcome, they used their favorite excerpts from his book (which they ran by him first via email).

Simran read aloud from Dr. Roberts' autobiography:

I had walked to the Crystal Burger, a hamburger joint in Little Rock where my favorite order was burger, fries, and chocolate malt—to go. The Crystal Burger was a white-owned establishment. I had been there many times before, and I knew the rules very well. . . . Black people could not eat the food they had purchased while still inside the Crystal Burger; they could not occupy any of the counter stools or chairs around the tables; they could only order food to go. . . .

This day was no different except that right after placing my order, I hopped up on one of the stools at the counter to wait for my burger and fries. It was most certainly out of character for me to do that. I don't remember why I decided to sit on the stool that day. It just felt like an ordinary thirteen-year-old kind of thing to do while I waited . . . Suddenly there was absolute silence. . . . I had forgotten the script.

Figure 6.5 Dr. Roberts shares his lessons from Little Rock.

Then Jina continued the introduction:

"On September 4, 1957, Terrence Roberts and eight other African American students (known as the 'Little Rock Nine') made an unsuccessful attempt to enter Little Rock Central High School in Little Rock, Arkansas. Despite the presence of the National Guard, an angry crowd of about four hundred white people surrounded the school.

"Nineteen days later the students again attempted to enter the school while surrounded by a mob of a thousand people. The following day, President Dwight D. Eisenhower sent U.S. Army troops to accompany the students to the school for protection. The troops were stationed at the school for the entirety of the school year, although they were unable to prevent incidents of violence inside.

"In 1999, Dr. Roberts and the other members of the Little Rock Nine were awarded the Congressional Gold Medal by President Bill Clinton.

"Now we would like to invite Dr. Roberts to the stage to share with us his Lessons from Little Rock."

Sometimes kids' questions get answered easily with a text or a web resource, what we call "quick-finds." Sometimes the questions require more in-depth research. And, in some cases, questions can only be answered by including opinions, beliefs, values, and, most of all, experience. The beauty of having an expert as a resource, especially one who has lived through some history, is that you get the full package. Taking the time to send out an email or pick up the phone can lead to transformative insights for your students. Relationships are forged and the life lessons are invaluable.

In Figure 6.6, see kids in Laura Olson's classroom interviewing the United States Olympic luge team. A reminder: Accomplished and even famous adults love to help kids learn.

Figure 6.6 U.S. Olympic luge team visits Laura Olson's fifth graders at Eason Elementary School.

7

Pursue Kids' Own Questions with Mini-Inquiries

why

Providing time for kids to investigate their own questions allows us to honor their curiosity, to spark engaging and authentic inquiries, and to model for them how experienced researchers seek answers. We realize that children often come up with questions that are more profound, more interesting, and sometimes, more charmingly original than we grown-ups would ever think of.

what
We Might Say to Kids

"What a great question! I don't know much about that myself. Shall we take some time and look into it? Or come back to it later this week? Right now? OK, put away those books for a few minutes and let's dig in."

how
Long It Might Take

Five minutes for a quick-find on a right-answer topic; longer for more complex questions. Mini-inquiries have the potential to lead to extended inquiries into deep topics. Genius Hour doesn't have to be exactly an hour, and kids can carry Genius Hour projects across many weeks.

n previous chapters, we talked about how to elicit and bank kids' questions by having children record them in wonder books or journals and by collectively creating wonder walls filled with questions that individuals or groups can return to at any time. And we've seen how many teachers find time, daily or weekly, to return to those captured questions and help kids tackle them.

Now, we move a step further from teacher control and closer to student choice and responsibility. Kids' curiosity topics come front and center. We set aside time *right now*, and say, "I have been teaching you some stuff for a while. Now what do *you* want to learn about?"

Try This

Take a look back at Chapter 1, where you made a list of topics you were personally curious about. If you don't have it, take a minute now and jot down five or ten specific curiosities that you are currently carrying around. These questions should be reasonably meaty, not just factual quick-finds (e.g., How old is Taylor Swift?). If you are reading this book as part of a teacher study group, you can support each other to find rich categories and topics. Got a bunch in mind?

Next, choose one of your own wonders and give yourself fifteen minutes to dig into it. Like right now. Google it, read about it, run to the library, interview someone, phone a friend—do whatever it takes to generate some information and answers. When you are done, talk or reflect on the process.

I trust you found it fun and interesting to pursue a mini-inquiry of your own. If your topic was big enough, you probably have more questions now than you did fifteen minutes ago—and you might be looking for time to continue your investigation. Which is exactly what we find so many kids doing when they jump into mini-inquiries in class.

Last spring at Glenwood School, Christina Jepsen had no plans for her kindergartners to deeply investigate bees. But since everything was blooming around the school, she invited her kiddos to create art and writing for a "Spring Book." While they worked, one student came over and asked, "What color are bees' wings?" Others started piping in and guessing. Somebody shouted "Yellow!" So Christina had everyone come over and look up bees on the computer. They learned a fancy new word, *transparent*. Then another student said that bees die when they sting you—but others said no. The Bee-Quest was off and running.

During her next prep time, Christina made a chart: Bees Can, Bees Have, and Bees Are (see Figure 7.1). Meanwhile, coach Deb Zaffiro quickly pulled some bee books from the library and the bookroom. Christina created extra time that afternoon for partners to dive into some bee information and gave them sticky notes to capture their findings. Kids filled them up with bee facts and posted them in the appropriate column on the chart. Among their findings:

Bees Can: fly, buzz, make honey, with their tongues drink nectar, build honeycombs, make hives

Bees Have: big eyes, stingers, transparent wings, antennae

Bees Are: blue, red, yellow, black, and green

Figure 7.1
Kindergarten chart for collecting bee information

Even later that day, many kids were still reading, writing, and making bee art. Christina and Deb were almost glad for the day to bee over!

Sometimes in these mini-inquiries, kids surprise us not just with their curiosity, but with their caring. In Peoria, Illinois, this past year, a new student arrived at Mark Bills Middle School. Deaf since birth, Rhemy Elsey had spent his previous years in a special school for hearing-impaired children. But now, at age eleven, his mom felt he was ready for regular school. The kids welcomed Rhemy, but hadn't had close contact with a person with hearing loss before. He used sign language, which none of them understood, with his in-class translator, Tammy Alvin. The kids became concerned that they couldn't communicate with Rhemy as well as they would like.

With open inquiries, we unleash our trust in kids. We invite them to lavish their wonder on the world. We set up just as much structure as kids need to succeed, and not one scaffold more.

So Desyrae Clark and Tabria Smith went to the principal with an idea. They wanted permission to start an American Sign Language (ASL) class, so they could learn to communicate with Rhemy. By early October, a voluntary group of eleven students was spending every Wednesday, during lunch and recess, meeting with Rhemy to learn his way of talking. Desyrae summed it up for a visiting reporter: "Instead of learning a foreign language like Spanish or French that I can use in the future, I wanted to learn sign language so that I can use it right now to speak to Rhemy" (Zaslow 2016).

With these more open mini-inquiries, we unleash our trust in kids. We invite them to lavish their wonder on the world, near and far, pedestrian and profound, age-appropriate and precocious, self-centered and empathic. We set up just as much structure as they need to succeed, and not one scaffold more. As you'll see in the models that follow, this doesn't mean we become observers; indeed, there is as much art in facilitating research as there is in presenting content.

SCHEDULE A GENIUS HOUR
Set aside time for kids to investigate

Daniel Argyres, fourth-grade teacher at Glenwood School

Every Friday from 2:30 to 3:30, Daniel Argyres' fourth graders enjoy a whole hour to pursue their own curiosity questions. Much like employees in today's most progressive, high-tech companies, these kids are trusted to create valuable (if not necessarily profitable) ideas and products on their own for part of the week.

Daniel says that managing the actual hour is pretty straightforward, and we'll see his organizational strategies shortly. But what he most carefully cultivates is the quality and abundance of the questions kids bring to Genius Hour. To ensure that Genius Hour is really *geniusy*, Daniel plans activities all week long that help kids surface and record possible topics for Friday afternoon. As Daniel explains, there are four ways he makes sure kids develop good questions for their "free inquiry" on Fridays.

I Model My Own Genius Hour Questions

Once or twice a week, I gather the students on the rug and sit with them. I bring along my Inquiry Journal and talk about my own current interests, questions, and findings [see Figure 7.2]. I show them my list of curiosity/wonder questions—usually twenty or thirty items I am working on—clearly numbered and organized [Figure 7.3]. I'll often show students the research I conducted on one particular question. One of my topics (the Battle of Thermopylae)—kept me busy for three weeks! After seeing

Figure 7.2 Daniel Argyres shares his curiosity journal with his fourth graders.

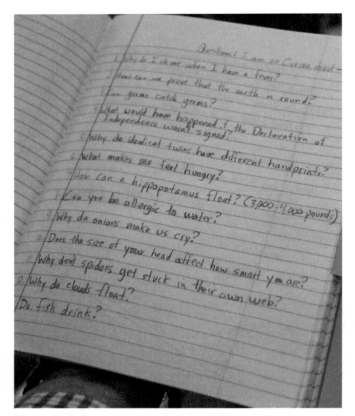

Figure 7.3 Some wonders in Daniel's journal

my research, photos, diagrams, and such the students really begin to understand research dedication and knowledge acquisition. And we need lots of worthy questions, some for a single Genius Hour, and others we can pursue for days or weeks.

Kids Keep Curiosity Lists in Journals

Following my example, students maintain lists of questions/wonders/curiosities in their own Inquiry Journals. To keep better track of their curiosity, I have the kids number their wonders, just like I do. As they research a question and become confident in their newfound knowledge, they can check it off. This small requirement has helped a lot of kids to organize their thoughts, plan their research time more

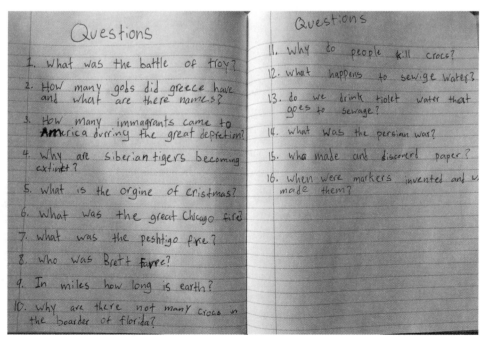

Figure 7.4 Pages from Peyton's Learning Journal

effectively, and remain focused on one big topic at a time. Figure 7.4 shows a couple of pages from Peyton's Inquiry Journal from last year.

Just in case you can't decipher those faint pencil marks in the photo, here are some of Peyton's topics:

How many gods did the Greeks have and what were their names?

How many immigrants to America in the great depression?

Why are Siberian tigers becoming extinct?

What is the origin of Christmas?

What was the Peshtigo fire?

What happens to sewage water?

Do we drink toilet water that goes to sewage?

Why are there not many crocodiles in the border of Florida?

Why do people kill crocs?

Who made and discovered paper?

When were markers invented and who made them?

As you see, there are plenty of thick and rich inquiry questions here (as well as some correctable misconceptions) that Jack can spend many Genius Hours investigating.

Use a Curiosity Chart and Question Boxes

Another way to spark classroom curiosity (and prepare for our weekly Genius Hour) is by maintaining a "What Are You Curious About?" anchor chart. Of course, kids are welcome to post a question any time they are passing by. But we also set aside a time once a week when we gather specifically to brainstorm ideas for the wonder wall. We all meet briefly on the rug with a sticky note and a pencil. Either on their own or working with a buddy, the students generate thick, thought-provoking questions, read them aloud, and stick them on the curiosity chart as we move to our next activity [see Figure 7.5].

We also have two Wonder Boxes displayed in the room [Figure 7.6]. Throughout the day, students are encouraged to write any burning question/ thought/curiosity on index cards and place them in a Wonder Box. It's a great place for kids to contribute a question they don't feel comfortable raising in

Figure 7.5 Curiosity chart in fourth grade

Figure 7.6 Wonder Boxes for storing great inquiry questions

front of everyone—or just to surprise their classmates later. On Friday, when we open the Wonder Boxes, the questions we find there can help kids who are still shopping for a Genius Hour topic.

POINT OUT

You might be thinking, man, this almost looks like curiosity overkill! But what Daniel guarantees is that kids are noticing and capturing their wonders all week long—providing an abundance of choices for everyone when Genius Hour arrives.

Coming to Genius Hour

As we begin, I read aloud the questions on the curiosity chart. Even though these have been accumulating all week, reading them aloud adds value. Kids love hearing their questions read publicly—it gives them ownership of their learning and makes them feel empowered to pursue that question. And it makes some topics come alive that might otherwise have been neglected. When I notice overlapping topics, I encourage those students to work together for "double the learning power." Next, we have a brief brainstorming period during which we open up the Wonder Boxes and share their contents for anyone who is still topic shopping. And of course there are always the kids' learning journals to draw upon. Once everyone is set with their topics, off we go.

I give kids the option of working with a partner on a shared question, or individually on their own. I often encourage partnerships based on similar interests among students. I release the kids to find learning areas that will be most productive to their kind of research. Some choose to work at a table in the back, while others prefer the front carpet or their own desk. The students investigate their chosen question using books, articles, technology (using safe Internet search engines), working hard to become knowledgeable on that topic. I ask them to record facts, diagrams, and other valuable information in their Inquiry Journals.

My role during Genius Hour is to confer, facilitate, encourage, direct, and offer feedback throughout the process. During the week, I have been meeting with students to discuss their research questions, making sure they are on the right track for this Friday. That also means I have already found out some of the topics students will be researching Friday, so I can gather materials ahead of time. As I range through the room, I have a checklist on a clipboard that keeps the students (and me) accountable. It has three columns: Student Name, Topic Choice, and Task Completed. I carry that around with me and jot entries as I meet with students, making notes on their progress/concerns. Some investigations are completed in one week's Genius Hour, but kids often work on a single topic over several weeks.

The students really get into Genius Hour when it's modeled, managed appropriately, and has set guidelines. Some of my fourth graders' recent Genius Hour inquiries included:

- What is Alcatraz Island?

- Why did the Battle of Thermopylae occur?

- What if we were born old and died young?

- What were the orphan trains like during the 1920s and what happened if children were abandoned?

- Is there life on other planets, and if so, how do we really know?

- Why do I shiver when I have a fever?

- How does the human body *really* work?

I encourage the students to dive deep. They constantly hear me say: "Go for quality, not quantity. Following your research, you should be able to answer your question and become an expert on that topic." Encouraging the students to really dig in and focus on one amazing question allows them to unleash their creative energy and engage in their topic wholeheartedly.

Near the end of Genius Hour, the students gather on the rug and I have as many as possible read their question and share three to five important facts they learned from their research. The sharing portion often carries over until Monday's Morning Meeting simply because I want each student or group to take pride in their work, share their learning, and feed the community with ideas for future inquiries.

BANK KIDS' QUESTIONS FOR FUTURE INVESTIGATIONS
Open the destination jar

Darcy Nidey, fourth-grade teacher at Eason Elementary School

Figure 7.7 Travel Tuesdays destination jar

At Eason Elementary School, the fourth-grade teachers run a recurring inquiry project called "Travel Tuesdays." In Darcy Nidey's room, it begins the first week of school; she asks kids to think about the one place in the whole wide world that they would most like to visit someday. She gives students plenty of time to think it over and talk with buddies before deciding. Then, the kids write their dream destination on a tiny piece of paper, fold it up, and ceremonially drop it in a big glass jar (see Figure 7.7). Darcy places the jar on a high shelf and tells kids that every Tuesday all year long, they will draw out one slip of paper, and then investigate the destination named on the paper. Each student's travel question will become a whole-class inquiry in due course—but just once a week until the jar is empty.

By the time I visit Eason Elementary in early spring, there are only a few destinations left when Darcy lifts the jar down from the shelf. With all the kids on the rug in front of her, and with great drama, Darcy extracts one of the few remaining slips of paper. After slow unwrapping and a long pause, she reads: "Alaska!" Kids laugh and high-five—a popular topic, tucked away months ago by one of their classmates.

Jumping into the near future, I can tell you that *four minutes and thirty seconds from now*, every student will be hard at work, researching a self-chosen topic about Alaska, most of them working with partners who have similar questions.

With inquiry projects we sometimes spend too much time setting things up. And if we slow down too much, kids can lose energy and start complaining. See how Darcy makes it brisk, crisp, and efficient.

POINT OUT

Start the clock. Darcy hands out a four-quadrant note-taking form where kids use the first two boxes to write down (1) what they already know about today's destination and (2) some questions they have about it. The other boxes are for jotting down information they find from at least two sources later on. The students immediately start jotting about their background knowledge—they have done this before. I am surprised when no more than a minute later, Darcy tells them to go ahead and write one burning question about Alaska in the second box. Already?

Another minute later, she calls students to attention. Now Darcy wants the kids to state their research topics so she can help them find a partner if they want one, and move off the rug ASAP.

This process went by really fast, but here's what I heard (get a glimpse in Figure 7.8):

Darcy: OK, who has a topic?

Student: Alaskan animals.

Darcy: You mean pick one and research it? Got one in mind?

Student: Bears.

Darcy: Who wants bears? One, two, three. OK, grab a computer, find a place to work, and dig in! Who's next?

Student: Who lives there?

Darcy: People of Alaska, great topic; you two, go! Emmy, what have you got?

Student: What do the people eat?

Darcy: Hmm, foods of Alaska? Anyone else? Nobody? Looks like you're on your own, Em. Find your spot.

Student: Mountains.

Darcy: What about them?

Students: Mountain climbing. Mt. McKinley. Old volcanoes.

Darcy: Mountains, OK, looks like you three have different subtopics, so you might want to work on your own, but sit near each other as a resource. Go ahead, you guys.

Student: Alaska cruises.

Darcy: Ha! I might get into that group! OK, two for cruises, off you go.

Student: Glaciers.

Darcy: Just glaciers?

Student: We were wondering about are they melting, climate change?

Darcy: Sounds good, grab a computer and find your space.

A couple more negotiations like these and the rug is empty. *Elapsed time: Four minutes and thirty seconds.*

Now Darcy goes to her own computer, opens a Padlet page, and makes a box for each research team, labeling it with the kids' names and their chosen Alaska topic. (You

Figure 7.8 Darcy Nidey helps kids pick topics and form groups.

could also do this on big chart paper, with kids posting their findings by placing sticky notes in designated boxes.) This stays projected on the classroom screen for the rest of the inquiry time, and it gradually fills up with information as the kids switch from raw note taking to synthesizing and posting their findings.

Darcy is now operating in coaching mode, swinging by teams and individuals, reading screens over kids' shoulders. She offers a comment here, suggests a search term there. Her touch is light. Kids are now using the other two boxes on their note-taking forms, filling in information from at least two different sources. At this point, it's OK to copy down key words and phrases from whatever they're reading. The final step is to synthesize the most important things they have learned and type it up for the Padlet on the screen (see Figure 7.9).

I go and sit with Emily, who's investigating "what Alaskans eat" on her own. Just as I slide up, she quite reasonably googles "Alaska food" and the first hit she gets is—wait for it—baked Alaska! She looks at me like, What just happened? I explain that this is a fancy dessert that I have eaten a couple of times, but I don't think it's really a common food of Alaskans. We talk about the difference between food that might be *served* in Alaska (including McDonald's fries) and food that is *grown* or *produced* there. When Em starts looking up "Alaska fish," I figure she's on a good track and slip away to work with the bear boys, who are sitting under the screen.

I come back to Em just in time to see her posting to her Padlet box:

Some sea foods they eat are walrus, seal, whale, halibut, salmon, clams, oysters, and most importantly, crab. Alaskans find a lot of berries. Some of these berries are salmonberries, lingonberries, which are cousins to the cranberry, and mossberries which can be turned into jelly. . . .

Within twenty minutes, Em and her classmates have learned tons of information about Alaskan animals, mountains, glaciers, cruises, and more. There's no big ceremony, no need for a whole class gathering. The kids are happy to share what they have learned with the kids around them—and then look forward to next week's Travel Tuesday. (Figure 7.10 shows kids pursuing another week's investigation.)

Caleb-Matanuska Glacier

The Metanuska is the largest Glacier reachable by vehicle in the entire USA. It is a very famous Glacier in Alaska, and is ranked as the 2nd best place there. Being extremely big, it is 27 miles long, and has a Terminus (front-to-back) of 4 miles. It is known as a "Valley Glacier" and a "Weather hole," which I am guessing is from the way it is made, like a hole in the ground.

Keon–Alaskan volcanos

There was a volcanic eruption in Alaska that sent the clouds of ash it was so bad for Alaska people did not like that it is terrible a lot of people don't even go by it any more.

What traditional food they have—Emily

Some sea foods they eat are walrus, seal, whale, halibut, salmon, clams, oysters, and most importantly, crab. Alaskans find a lot of berries. Some of these berries are salmonberries, lingonberries which are cousins to the cranberries, and mossberries which can be turned into jelly centers sometimes they can be called crowberries. Salmonberries are made into basically the same things as the mossberries.

What and how do wolfs live in Alaska and what is there lifestyle? Afton

I learned a lot about wolves and I am going to tell you what wolves behave and act like. Wolves are very active and they hunt seals and fish.

Ayohnna: Do they have bears if so what kind?

There are three kinds of bears. The polar, black, grizzly/brown. The black bear is the smallest and the most command. The brown bear's favorite thing to eat is salmon. Polar bears have small heads which leads to smaller ears and teeth. they are about the same size as the grizzly/brown bear.

Kjersten—Leather Back Sea Turtles

Leather Back Sea Turtles limbs are designed specially for swimming. Their front flippers are larger then their back flippers. Leather Backs do not have bony plates on their shells like other sea turtles. In 1970 they were listed as endangered. Their average life span is about 45 years. They can be as long as 7 feet. The largest sea turtle ever found was 2,020 pounds.

Oliver—What is Alaska's population compared to other states or cities?

Alaska's population is 736,732 as of 2014. Did you know one of Alaska's city's Anchorage is almost half of Alaska's population. Anchorage is only 436,309 people apart from Alaska's population. Did you know that Rhode island

Maddi—What is the weather in Alaska?

For Travel Tuesday we were going to Alaska and my question was, What is the weather like in Alaska and here is what I found, the Summer months are June, July, August, May, and September. In Summer the temperature is usually 60 or 70 degrees. Sometimes the sun is out for 18–21 hours.

Figure 7.9 Padlet page showing kids' findings for Alaska inquiries

Figure 7.10 Kids work on another Travel Tuesday investigation. Destination this time: Denver, Colorado.

MAKE TIME FOR KIDS' CRAZIEST QUESTIONS
Peanut butter bandits

Sarah Van Lieshout, third-grade teacher at Glenwood School

No one is more attuned to kids' off-the-wall questions than third-grade teacher Sarah Van Lieshout at Glenwood School. Listen as she uncorks the saga of the Peanut Butter Bandits:

> During one of our morning soft starts, two students paired up to learn about diamonds. When time came to share our findings, this pair blurted out an astonishing fact they discovered: "You can make peanut butter into diamonds!" Wait, what? Of course, the entire class erupted with questions.
>
> We immediately began a "quick-find" search on the smartboard. I was modeling how to adjust and choose the best terms in a search engine. Unfortunately, not a single source could be found to confirm the bulletin about diamonds and peanut butter. Even worse, the partners could not remember the source of the original (alleged) fact! Which of course led to a conversation about the importance of keeping track of information and sources to support our ongoing research. Didn't anyone remember all those note-taking procedures we practiced?
>
> The class, including myself, chalked up the false factoid as a piece of Internet flotsam with no credibility. Most importantly, we realized we could

gobble the peanut butter sandwiches we brought for lunch without breaking a tooth—or missing out on a million-dollar opportunity.

Unsurprisingly, several other partnerships used their subsequent "soft start" time to continue the treasure hunt, determined to find the source of the PB=D combination. A few days later, we were all amazed when a group showed us a website that validated the claim! This time, they had remembered to write it down. Lesson learned. Teacher win! (If you google this topic now—and you should—you'll find dozens of references to the study, originally conducted by scientists at Germany's Bayerisches Geoinstitut).

POINT OUT

Listen as Sarah purposely uses adult-level material because there are no kid-level texts covering this topic. She and her kids dope out the text together, reading, drawing, and talking.

We displayed the article on our smartboard and tackled the technical chemistry terms and some complicated diagrams. After using "picture note taking" and physically acting out parts of the article, we gradually developed some understanding of the atomic structure of diamonds and their formation in environments with lots of heat and pressure. The scientists who did this research were not chemists (or chefs): they were geologists trying to re-create the conditions inside the Earth's lower mantle, where the temperature is 2,000 degrees Celsius and pressures are 1.3 million times higher than on Earth's surface. They figured out how to re-create the high pressure and temperatures, and then pressed peanut butter between two diamonds. This converted the atomic structure of the peanut butter into one similar to that of a diamond [see Figure 7.11]. And any other carbon material would probably work the same way. Wow!

Now, students burst into their readers' workshop to study chemistry textbooks, compare the atomic structure of rocks, and learn how crystals are formed. Many of these sources included vocabulary and concepts well above the students' background knowledge and (supposed) reading

Photo by Jurvetson (Flickr) and certified su (Flickr)

Figure 7.11 A magical combination?

levels. The Wisconsin state standards do not list the formation of crystalline structures as a third-grade topic. But where there is curiosity, there is a way!

You might wonder what I was *supposed* to be covering while this diamond inquiry unfolded. We were right in the middle of unit on mysteries in reading and one on persuasive text in writing—neither of which included the study of chemistry. I had to make some careful decisions to allow for exploration of an unplanned topic that galvanized kids, yet remain faithful to district pacing. I decided that following the kids' lead was worth a few missed lessons from our curriculum. Their work was proof that the risk paid off. I witnessed students transferring research skills from their science classroom and applying skills from a nonfiction reading unit that happened months before. Allowing students to spiral back to previous skills, while providing additional research practice through these spontaneous investigations, really did create independence and ownership of the research process.

When were finishing up our investigation of how peanut butter can be changed into diamonds, Mrs. Dixon's second-grade class across the hall just happened to be wrapping up their annual peanut butter drive for the local food bank. That made us a little suspicious: Did the second-grade teachers know all along?! And what did they *really* do with the peanut butter?! Some mutual spying broke out between the two rooms. Always on alert, my kids would holler a warning if they saw Mrs. Dixon skulking about. And she skulked a lot. Based on this rivalry, we dreamed up the notion that those evil second graders might be cooking up diamonds in their secret laboratory in our school's abandoned basement, with plans to one day buy the school and turn it into a secret spy agency! But if you want to know the whole story, you'll have to wait until we finish our cowritten storybook, *The Peanut Butter Bandits*, coming to your local bookstore soon!

Recently somebody leaned out a car window and photographed this sign beside the road. It's been retweeted over a million times.

Next time you are afraid to share your ideas,

remember someone once said in a meeting

let's make a movie with a tornado full of sharks.

Is it just me, or does this remind you of how deliciously off-the-wall (and stealthily profound) kids' wonderings can be?

In my own teaching, supporting mini-inquiries about my students' spontaneous questions is my very favorite role. Nothing makes me happier than doing a search-aloud for the class or sitting beside a kid and helping to investigate a subject I know absolutely nothing about. Maybe this kind of jumping off a cliff is an acquired taste; good thing we saved it for later in the book. Such mini-inquiries do require our willingness to say things like, "Ooops, that search didn't pan out" or "Let's try something else." But when we take this seeming risk, we are actually modeling for kids what real-life research looks like: it's not easy, straight line, or prebookmarked. Instead, inquiry is more likely to be a wandering, recursive path, with plenty of distracting side roads and occasional dead ends. When we show kids the real process, and how exciting it is, we help them fall in love with finding out.

8

Address Curricular Units with Mini-Inquiries

why

To build curiosity for a required curricular subject, especially one that does not immediately interest children. We solicit kids' questions about the topic and use these to drive the upcoming study.

what

"You know that we are going to be studying our state's history soon, right? Before we get started, let's try this . . ." Or, "Now that we have studied our state history, choose something you found especially interesting or curious and look into it further."

We Might Say to Kids

how

Ten to fifteen minutes at the start of a curricular unit. As subject unfolds, refer back and check off kids' questions. Or provide some time *after* a unit for kids to do their own research on lingering questions about the subject.

Long It Might Take

I n planning an upcoming unit, we have all asked ourselves, "How am I gonna get the kids hooked on this?" When the subject is insects or extreme weather, no worries, but when it is New Mexico (or any state's) history, students may not be frothing with anticipation. At one level, this hooking process is a teacher gut/commonsense notion: if you can get kids interested in a topic at the beginning, that energy can carry them through a whole unit. This instinct has now been validated by research showing that curiosity and interest are triggerable states of mind (see page xxii, and Harvey and Daniels 2015). In other words, if we can flip on that "curiosity switch" in the brains of our students, we empower them to grapple, persist, and build knowledge on topics they would never have chosen on their own. In Figure 8.1, we see a teacher setting up a mandated curricular unit by helping kids list their questions about the subject first.

For about twenty years, I was a "teacher educator," meaning that I taught new teachers. Here's how I began discussions about planning in my classes: Look ahead into that dry, boring unit you have to teach and find the one most fascinating, weird, disgusting, bizarre, puzzling, amazing, funky thing about it. Regardless of when it would normally appear in the curricular sequence, bring it to the front, and start with that. Studying Native Americans? Show kids how the Pueblo Indians expelled the Spanish colonists from their territory after eighty years of occupation. Got a unit on immigration? Hand around some artifacts and pictures from a real family's trip though Ellis Island. Studying electricity? Show kids how Edison publicly electrocuted animals, including an elephant, to prove the superiority of his direct current. (OK, maybe save that one for middle school.)

Figure 8.1
Glenwood School, a
hothouse of learning

Try This

Identify a subject you "have to teach" during the school year, maybe one that kids have snoozed through in the past. You're looking for a chunk of curriculum that hasn't been the kids' favorite—or yours either. Got it?

Now look deeper into this unit, using the lens we just talked about—try to find the one most interesting, crazy, stunning, or unexpected aspect or story that you could use as a hooking device for your kids. This probably does not mean looking through the textbook (if there is one) or the curriculum guide. What you want to do is search on the web, probably beginning with *adult* resources, and then adapting them back to your kids.

One sure-fire example: for that stultifying state history unit, google a phrase like "weird (fill in your state) history." If you type in Texas, for example, you'll find some odd laws.

In Texas, it's against the law for anyone to have a pair of pliers in his or her possession.

In Texas, it is still a "hanging offense" to steal cattle.

In Texas, you may not shoot a buffalo from the second story of a hotel.

In Corpus Christi, it is illegal to raise alligators in your home.

In Galveston, it is illegal to have a camel run loose in the street.

Alternatively, you can let the kids dig into what they find interesting *after* you've addressed the required subject matter.

When Sara Ahmed had to teach a required topic to her fifth or sixth graders, she'd have them keep track of any unanswered questions or puzzling details during the official unit. Then she'd save some class time later for kids to investigate their own wonderings about the curricular topic. Sara says this "backloading" was especially effective because by this time, kids had already learned so much about the subject that they could choose a more focused and sustainable question to pursue.

Now, let's visit several classrooms where teachers are prepping kids for curricular topics by using brief mini-inquiries.

PROVOKE CHILDREN'S CURIOSITY WITH YOUR OWN STORY
Scary tornadoes

Kari Ridolfi, kindergarten teacher at Burley School

Kari Ridolfi had a weather unit coming up in her Chicago kindergarten. While it isn't too tough to get five-year-olds excited about weather, Kari knew they'd be really hooked when she told them a scary and exciting true-life story at Monday's morning meeting.

While driving to visit her grandparents in Wisconsin, Kari and her husband drove through a terrible storm. Suddenly there were tornado sirens, golf-ball-sized hail, and bright green skies. They had to pull over under a bridge to take cover, where they stayed for almost an hour. As it turns out, a tornado touched down in a city nearby. It was then that Kari realized she knew next to nothing about how tornadoes formed and roared over the land.

"I shared my story with the students, whose wide eyes were brimming with questions, worry, and wonder," says Kari. "As I modeled my own curiosities about tornadoes, lively conversations immediately erupted." Kari got out a piece of chart paper and the children used sticky notes to write down their wonders (see Figure 8.2). As the chart filled up, Kari decided to launch a mini tornado inquiry.

Figure 8.2 Kids post their questions about tornadoes.

The students broke into groups based on their burning questions. They gathered books and magazines about tornadoes from the classroom library. Kari had marked some important pages with sticky notes. She and the students also printed some diagrams, maps, and images of tornadoes from online resources. Each group created a basket filled with resources and got right to work. The room was buzzing with excitement as students recorded their new learning, using combinations of pictures and words, on "think sheets"—two-column forms where students recorded research information on the left side and their new questions (which kept bubbling up) on the right (see Figure 8.3). Kari recalls, "From an outsider's view, the room probably looked chaotic. Papers were scattered everywhere and dog-eared pages lined the tables. But inquiry work with thirty-one kindergartners is *always* joyfully messy."

Figure 8.3 Wonderings and learnings about tornadoes

As Kari knelt down to talk with each group, a common thread kept reappearing. Safety. The kids all wanted to learn more about being protected from a tornado. So after they came back as a whole group, she knew that was where the inquiry needed to focus next. Once the whole-group share of new learning was complete and lingering questions were highlighted and added to the wonder wall, they started to zoom in on tornado safety.

So often with inquiry, we hear the questions kids have beneath their questions. Among the most common are topics that make children wonder: Am I safe? Will I be OK? Could this happen here? To me? To us?

POINT OUT

Kari handed each student a whiteboard, and they recorded their feelings about tornadoes. They also recorded things that could be done to make them feel OK about these dangerous storms. Through conversation, Kari was able to scribe a whole-class list of next steps for investigation. "The students wanted to write a letter to the principal asking about the school's tornado drill protocol. We also drafted a letter home to parents so they could make a 'tornado plan' at home, too. With that, their work for the morning was done. The students were bursting with information about tornadoes and had an understanding about what would happen if a tornado touched down in Chicago. Within a few short days, there was a plan for what would happen if a tornado came near our school, along with many plans that were drafted by families."

Kari put all of the work that was completed that morning, along with the safety plan drafts, onto a bulletin board called "Tracking Tornadoes." The children also turned the dramatic play area into a weather center filled with binoculars, raincoats, tornado books, calendar images, pens, pencils, notepads, toolboxes, and more. If a tornado were to come to Chicago, these five-year-olds would be the first ones to know. And they would know exactly what to do.

USE STUDENTS' QUESTIONS TO SET UP A CURRICULAR TOPIC

Electricity quick-finds

Mary Beth Hes and **Heather Greene**, third-grade teachers at Duke School

For years, as part of Duke School's project-based curriculum, teachers have collected the students' questions early on in their science and social studies projects and continued to gather them throughout each study. The broad outlines of these projects are teacher planned, but children's questions shape the direction of the inquiry all the way along. Here's how Mary Beth and Heather start with a question-recording meeting in third grade:

We listen to kids' conversations and questions throughout a project. When the time is ripe, we gather the class on the rug to harvest those questions. We give the students time to brainstorm with a turn and talk and call on children to share their questions. It's exciting to see the students piggyback off each other's wonderings as one question inspires another.

Here's a sample of what our children wondered at the start of our electricity project:

How does a battery work?

How is electricity created?

Do faucets use electricity?

Why does static make things cling to each other?

Does a smartboard use electricity?

What are the parts needed to produce electricity?

We always post the students' questions prominently in the classroom, and many of them get answered along the way through our projects. However, in past years, there was no formal process in place to investigate students' lingering wonderings and to document the answers to their questions as they developed new understandings.

This year, we were inspired to carve out time to delve more deeply into the children's wonderings. We dedicated a couple blocks of time during our multiweek electricity unit to researching these "quick-finds." Students were so motivated to do this research that they borrowed ten or fifteen minutes here and there for their investigations, such as during "settle in" first thing in the morning, during class job time after recess, and when they completed assignments early.

In the past, our chart of questions was often hung high above a bulletin board, out of reach. We decided it was time to make the kids' questions more physically accessible. So we strung a clothesline across our windows and posted questions individually on large pieces of paper. When students were inspired to research a question, they put their names on a sticky note next to the question. The children often did their research in pairs, and typed the answers to their questions on a shared Google Doc. We printed their findings and posted them below the original question.

Parents were able to admire the kids' research when they attended our project culmination a few weeks later. We heard compliments from the parents such as: "I am so impressed with how much the children know about this topic" and "I never did anything like this when I was in school!" Our very favorite comment to hear was, "Well, I certainly learned something today!"

POINT OUT

Notice that students are displaying their findings for two audiences—a casual sharing with classmates, and a formal exhibition for visiting parents. Like many inquiry schools, Duke School holds parent nights focused on kids' projects and their learning.

Some of the students' questions, such as how electricity is produced and how static cling works, were answered through our whole-class investigations or by guest specialists who visited the classroom. For other questions, like how a battery works and whether a faucet uses electricity, we were able to pull video, Internet, and book resources to answer them. Some questions the students were able to research independently, while others required adult guidance.

At our project culmination, some of the toughest questions—such as "What is a nuclear magnet and how does it work?"—remained unanswered. This reflects beautifully the reality that, in our world, there is no "end" to answering questions, and much of the joy of inquiry is in the process of investigation, rather than just gathering information. Our knowledge base grows over time and isn't contained to one project study at school. We have had a blast watching our students' curiosity unfold and observing their pride in the knowledge they now possess.

USE INQUIRY TO SPARK NONFICTION WRITING PRACTICE
The rules of the game

Brian Murphy, fourth-grade teacher at Disney 2 Magnet School

Quick inquiry projects are not limited to self-contained classrooms. "Specials" teachers (art, music, physical education) also love to jump on the inquiry bandwagon, and they often have creative ideas that we regular grade-level teachers would *never* think of.

When I was working at Disney 2 Magnet School in Chicago, the district had mandated that there must be writing in every class, every day. While this gave the regular classroom teachers something to think about, it was a real conundrum for the "specials" faculty.

PE teacher Brian Murphy came up with a writing-intensive mini-inquiry lesson for his fourth graders. Before kids arrived in the gym the next day, Brian emptied equipment closets, pulling out every sports and exercise object in the inventory: multisized balls, cones, rings, nets, foam tubes, hula hoops, poly spots, juggling scarves, duct tape, and bozo buckets. Then Brian opened some big plastic bags from Michaels craft store, where he had gone the night before to pillage the Dollar Bin. He'd bought kush balls, finger puppets, crazy straws, glow sticks, stacking cups, and even a couple of cheesy, battery-powered plush toys called "Light Up Duckies."

Next, Brian divided the objects into eight random piles, spaced at intervals around the gym floor. Hung on the wall directly behind each pile was a big sheet of chart paper and a box of colored markers. When the fourth graders arrived, puzzled looks prevailed as they scanned the mysterious mounds of colorful, random objects.

"OK you guys, in a minute, each of you is going to choose one of these stations and go there to create a brand new game, working with some classmates. You have to figure out the rules of your original game and try playing it enough to make sure it works. Then, you'll make a poster with the rules, and hang it on the wall. Finally, you'll use your poster to help you teach the game to at least one other group and some of the teachers who are visiting us in the gym today."

"One last thing. I want you to go to the station that has the most interesting objects *to you*, where you can be the most creative. So don't just follow your friends, go to where you can do something really original. OK, you're off!"

Brian allowed about twenty minutes for teams to create their games and write their rules poster. The hardest part was testing out objects, placements, and rules so the game was actually playable—and could be clearly explained on the poster. One group of boys kept it simple, taping plastic cups to the end of sticks and making up a lacrosse-like game in which you scored by passing a rubber ball from cup to cup and advancing through a cone-marked goal line. Another group created a sprawling Disney-esque fantasy game, where the players advanced through seven incredibly complex mini-worlds. Moving from level five to level six, for example, involved throwing a Light Up Duckie to another player. If it happened to light up during its flight, you advanced to the next fantasy—if not, you remained stuck on your current island.

Finally, the fifteen teachers who had been quietly watching from around the perimeter stepped in and let the kids teach them their games. There were howls of laughter, shouts of victory, and occasional disputes, which forced some teams to run back and revise their rules. Gym, nonfiction writing practice, and higher-order thinking—what a combination! Next day in writing class, the perfect topic appears: What factors make a game fun to play?

Before, during, and after curricular units, we can make room for kids' questions in short chunks of time. And as we experiment with this, we often find that even more of the subject matter can be "covered" in a kid-directed mode than we used to think. When students set their own questions, they very often assign themselves topics that were in the required curriculum anyway. In preparation for a unit on the sun and the moon, one third-grade class listed these questions:

Where did the moon come from?

How do eclipses happen?

Will the sun ever burn out?

Why does the moon change?

Why did Columbus think the world was flat?

Why do we get tan in summer?

Why does the Big Dipper move?

Why do we have seasons?

Left to their own investigations, these kids are primed to meet the state standards, and then some.

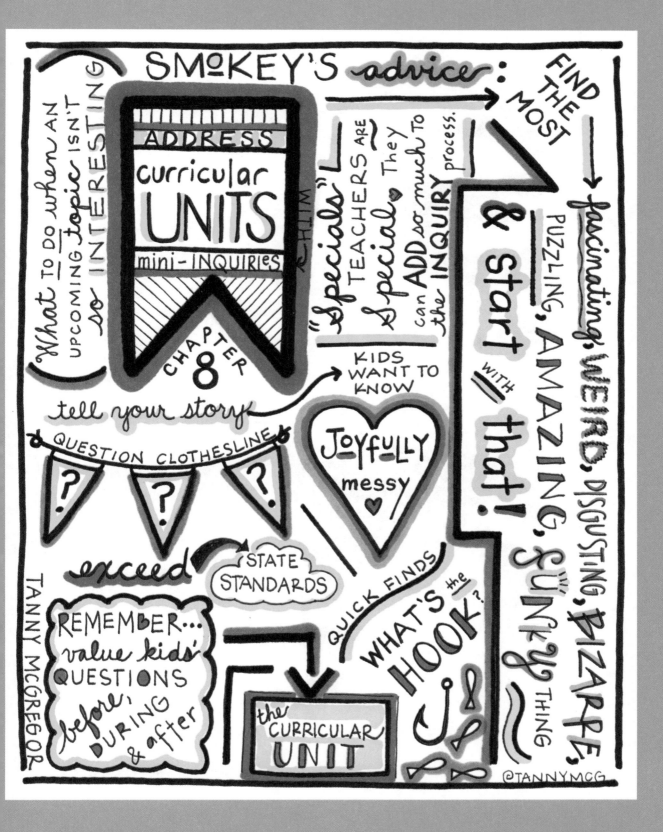

9

Lean into a Crisis

why

Crises, small and large, happen in our classrooms every year. We react to these events first from our hearts, and then by using inquiry strategies to help kids cope, build understanding, and carry on in hope.

what
We Might Say to Kids

"I know you guys may be feeling upset and worried today. I am too. Shall we talk about it? What are you wondering? Are there things we need to do?"

how
Long It Might Take

There are no limits; everything depends on the challenge at hand. We balance between the need to explicitly work on these pressing issues as a community and our awareness that kids shouldn't marinate in sadness for too long.

When you live with thirty other human beings for 180 days in a row, sad things and bad things can happen. Individual children or the whole group will encounter struggles, worries, losses, changes, or emergencies. It's not whether, but when.

Many of these happenings are predictable and expectable. A class pet dies. (Come to think of it, if you decide to have any classroom pets—whether hermit crabs, goldfish, birds, or guinea pigs—you are guaranteed to be conducting a funeral sometime during the year.) Then someone breaks a bone. Someone moves away. Someone new arrives. Someone has a sick parent or grandparent. Someone's family is in a car crash. There's a bullying incident on the playground. A big storm rages through town. There's scary news on TV and adults are agitated about it.

What all these sudden events have in common is that they *preempt the curriculum.* You and the kids have to deal with them immediately. They are not postponable; you can't do some planning over the weekend and then talk about someone's house burning down three days later. The issue, the problem, the worry, is on everyone's mind, preoccupying their thoughts, *right now.* You have to either actively suppress the topic or act. You can't play the expert because in these moments you usually don't have any more information than the children. As my colleague Robert Probst has written: "All of our teaching is in some ways preparation for such events" (2010).

We would not normally think of such situations as *entry points for inquiry*, and certainly not as *teachable moments.* First and foremost, we need to show our human empathy and concern, and partner with the children to manage their worries. But the tools and methods of inquiry—asking questions, gathering knowledge, listening to experts, considering alternatives, and working together to plan for action—are perfectly suited to this task. So what we *can* do is be an expert on helping kids think. If you are running an inquiry-style classroom, you have many assets already in place.

ZUMA Press, Inc./Alamy Stock Photo

Difficult news can pre-empt our teaching.

Try This

If you feel comfortable doing so, look back on some times when there was a crisis in a classroom where you were a student. This might have stemmed from scary world news, a community emergency, or something happening to a person in your own school or classroom.

Maybe you'll think of something like this: one day while goofing/flirting with some fourth-grade girls after lunch, I playfully tapped Audrey on the head with a textbook. She laughed and hit me back, but blood was already dripping down her forehead. I'd driven her cute pink barrette into her scalp, and she would soon be off to town for ten stitches. Meanwhile, totally horrified by what I had done, I was treated with complete sympathy by every adult around. The school nurse, perceiving an imminent breakdown, kindly laid me down for a nap until Audrey came back to show off her awesome (really big) bandage. Back in class, I am told, Mrs. Barnard discreetly scooped up all the blood-stained paper towels and helped my class deal with the crime scene and the sudden scare.

Once you identify one or more of these events, see what you can recollect about how your teacher managed. What did he or she say and do? What kinds of conversations were held, or what actions took place? Did you feel safe and comforted? Lost or in control? What memories do you carry from that time? Allow yourself to consider alternative teacher responses and how they may impact children during a crisis—and later on.

In this chapter, you'll hear how two teachers used the basic tools of inquiry learning to help their classes through some tough situations: the death of a classmate's parent and the fears engendered by frightening world events. Then, I'll offer a general model of how to support children through such emergencies, using the classic tools of inquiry that have already been introduced in the book. That guide is based on research in the mental health and social services community, as well as the several zillion years that my colleagues and I have been working with kids.

HELP KIDS RESPOND, FIND COMFORT, AND MAKE DECISIONS
When a classmate is hurting

Megan Dixon, second-grade teacher at Glenwood School

Last spring in Megan Dixon's second-grade classroom, a student's mother died suddenly. Due to the circumstances of the death and the family living situation, Megan knew she and John's classmates would have to play a large role in the healing process. After the funeral, a visit with the family, and a discussion with the school guidance counselor, they decided Megan would share the news with John's classmates before he returned to school. Since class meetings are a regular part of their classroom routines, Megan decided to bring up the subject during her next morning meeting.

After seventeen years as a classroom teacher, Megan has had the experience of working through the death of several classroom pets. "Standard protocol" includes reading *The Tenth Good Thing About Barney* by Judith Viorst, acknowledging sadness and other feelings students have, and sharing memories and "good things" about Fluffy, or Humphrey, or Oreo—orally and in writing. John's loss was of a different order of magnitude—and there was no protocol for a teacher to follow.

Megan spent the weekend reading about the grief children experience when losing a parent, dealing with loss in the classroom, and thinking about how to facilitate a class meeting on this sensitive topic. At first, she thought she would encourage children to share their feelings with comments such as "I'm so sorry about the loss of your mom." But then she wondered, what if all the children share at once and John becomes overwhelmed and further reminded of his loss? Maybe, she thought, we shouldn't say anything at all. Feeling uncertain and nervous about saying everything or nothing, Megan questioned how she could remain strong for her students and help them through this experience.

When a crisis or upsetting news allows us time, we can do our own research to make sure we have the facts right, to seek expert recommendations, and to grab materials that might help us work it through with the kids.

POINT OUT

As the students gathered for the class meeting, looking at her closely and sensing something very important was going to be shared, it became clear that Megan needed to trust her students more fully. She also needed to embrace her own sadness and be honest with her students that she did not have all the "right answers." She had to let kids talk, listen closely to their concerns, help them name their feelings, and guide them in creating personal or group action steps they could take when John returned.

She began the meeting by telling the students, "I have some very sad news and I've been struggling with how to tell you about it. . . . Many of you have wondered why John hasn't been here the past few days. The reason is that John's mom died. I know some of you who live near John already know this and have been very respectful by keeping this information private. I am very sad. I've been doing some reading about some things we can do to help John when he returns to school. . . . I know that I can trust you to help John and each other through this difficult time. You might be feeling sad, confused, or uncomfortable. That's OK. I have those feelings too. Let's share your thoughts and listen closely to each other with compassion."

Megan began by sharing what she learned from the resources she consulted over the weekend. She explained that other people who experienced a death like this wrote that teachers and students don't need to be experts. Instead, they can help most by being present and attentive to the grieving classmate and letting them express their feelings. Megan also explained that sometimes even though John is sad, he might not want to talk, and that's OK. A student chimed in that after her grandma died her mom didn't want to talk about it either.

She also shared that John would probably have a difficult time concentrating and learning for a while. She encouraged the students to "show patience and kindness and know that John may not participate in our activities the same way when he comes back." As expected with seven- and eight-year-olds, students began sharing stories of loss in their own lives. Perceiving that students needed a few moments to share these personal stories, Megan had students talk with their thinking partners about their own loss experiences. Some students talked about the death of pets, grandparents, and other relatives. After sharing some of these stories, Megan asked the second graders to think about what they might say to John when he returned.

As anticipated, the students knew they could probably say, "I'm sorry about your mom," but this didn't seem strong enough to convey the sadness they felt. They shared Megan's worry that if they all said the same words to John it wouldn't be meaningful enough or they would overwhelm him. One student even remarked, "If we all say we are sorry about your mom, that might remind John more of his mom and that could make him more sad." As students shared their feelings, they began problem solving and brainstorming. As they did this, Savanah suggested making a T-chart (a typical format for other instructional activities in this classroom) for what they could say and do. Students shared that they could say things like "I'm sorry," "You are a good friend," "I know how much you'll miss your mom." On the other side of the chart, they said they could give John a hug, smile at him, and make him pictures and cards.

POINT OUT Brainstorming and listing specific action steps gives worried children a feeling of comfort and control when the difficult events may last for a while.

As they continued the conversation, Megan found that some kids were worried that when John came back, they would be afraid to interact with him, might unconsciously shun him, and then he would feel isolated. So she started another round of brainstorming and listing: "Things we could do to be sure John doesn't feel alone tomorrow and throughout the week." These are some of the ideas kids came up with:

- walk with him to recess
- sit with him at lunch
- put dinosaur pictures in his mailbox
- fill his book bag with books he loves
- ask to be his partner during math

Megan finishes the story:

By the end of this process, every second grader had something unique and personal they could say to John, and a specific action they could take in welcoming him back the next day, and in the days that followed. Although no one felt expert at how to handle this, my students knew that they needed to be observers, exercise patience, and demonstrate empathy and understanding. For the next few weeks, that's exactly what happened. Students did respond with kindness and compassion in their words and actions. They were careful not to overwhelm John, but weren't scared to share their feelings.

John's mailbox overflowed with pictures and cards, and he was often seen reading and looking at them. At first, he would eat and have recess only in the classroom, but day by day he invited other students to join him as he worked his way back to more "normal" participation in everyday activities. He spent recesses and choice times drawing a variety of dinosaurs that adorned our classroom walls. He would carefully explain them—and his growing artistic expertise—to the class. Drawing seemed to be a way he dealt with much of his grief and how he shared his gratitude for his friends. He would often sneak dinosaur pictures he drew into other students' mailboxes, which were cherished by his classmates.

A month later, we were deeply saddened when John suddenly moved away to live with relatives in another town.

It was emotionally hard for Megan to prepare this story for publication, just a few months after the events. I'm grateful for her courage, both in the classroom and on the page. She is an extraordinary human being and a master teacher. I also think we can see in Megan's actions how she used the tools of inquiry to face this fraught situation. She:

- did her own research on the topic
- was authentic about her own thinking and feeling
- modeled her own ways of coping
- didn't assume an expert role
- acted as the lead learner in the room
- gathered kids as a community
- built upon previously established friendship and support
- created lessons based on kids' wonderings and worries
- let students speak and ask questions
- scribed students' thinking on charts
- helped children identify and plan possible actions
- supported kids to implement their plans over many days

When crises come to our classrooms, which they do, we must rely first on our hearts. But if we have already established a community of inquiry with our kids, we have ready at hand the structures we need to cope together.

ADDRESS AN UPSETTING NEWS EVENT
The world just handed us a curriculum

Sara Ahmed, instructional coach at NIST International School in Bangkok

There is always a piece of the curriculum that is unwritten. It cannot be planned out ahead or backwards-mapped later. It has no end-of-unit test.

This curriculum is handed to us by the world. We wake up to it before the school bell rings. We become aware that today's news will become tomorrow's history and it extracts an obligation from which we cannot look away.

Syria.

Dallas.

Orlando.

Newtown.

Paris.

Brussels.

Ferguson.

Chicago.

Baltimore.

Milwaukee.

St. Paul.

We become tense with names of cities, with headlines, with hashtags, with updates in 140 characters, with memes, and with graphic images of strangers across the sea or across the city.

In a world of 24/7 news reporting, where a bystander in Paris can bring breaking news to a kid in Harlem via Instagram, we live on a slippery slope between choosing to act and becoming desensitized.

But our classrooms are filled with twenty-five or thirty young identities, and the news stories and the worry come trickling down our halls and through our doors, onto our rug for morning meeting. The world hands us the curriculum once again [see Figure 9.1].

While visiting a school a while back, I had a very candid conversation with a fourth grader about one of the then-prospective presidential candidates.

The student turned to me and asked, "Can I ask you about Trump?"

Photo courtesy Pixabay

Figure 9.1 The world hands us a curriculum.

"What would you like to know?"

"Are you going to vote for him?"

Full hesitation to answer. "Well, do you want to discuss Trump as a candidate?"

"No. I just want to know if you are going to vote for him. He scares me."

"What scares you about him?"

"I'm Muslim. He hates Muslims."

Another student chimes in, "Yeah, he hates everyone. Even New Yorkers and he is from here."

From the mouths of nine-year-olds, an inquiry begins.

I didn't have a T-chart set up for comparing and contrasting candidates, nor did I have a preselected article ready to read with them. This piece of curriculum walked through the front door with the kids that morning. I talked with them a little more, but mostly listened to them get out their fears. I tried to instill some semblance of hope that they were being heard by a voting adult and that I would be sure to spread their message to my voting friends so they would hear the kids' voices also. I brought it up later with the principal, and he mentioned that kids as young as first and second grade expressed some fear of coming to school, of being teased by other students because they felt targeted by a potential candidate for president. This was a situation that was ripe for inquiry.

When world news has barged into my own classroom, I've relied on inquiry to help my students make sense of it. A few years ago, my students came into class disturbed by media images of mass graves of Syrian children. With genuine concern, the kids asked about what is being done to help the refugee children in Syria. I asked them: What should we do with all this worry? What would help them better understand the situation, and did they think there was anything we could do?

I set off to look for resources that night. On Twitter I came across the Karam Foundation, an organization that seemed to be kid-minded and working from awareness building to action. Next day, I told kids that I went home thinking about what they had said and did a little research for them and for me, to better understand what was going on with Syrian children. I gave them a link and asked them to brainstorm ways we could help.

Notice how much action Sara has taken here: general researching, finding and vetting a charity, and coming to school ready to propose that kids take some kind of action—but what kind? They must decide the details. That's teacher advocacy.

POINT OUT

The students were on fire. They read up on recent events in Syria and talked with the Karam Foundation's founders via email and Skype. Within days, the students had landed on a plan to make and sell bracelets to raise money for the foundation. They also planned to send bracelets to the kids at the foundation. As one of my students put it, "We are sending some money over there, and we are also making them a bracelet that we wear and that they wear, so they will know we are with them in spirit."

We made a YouTube video about our work and about what we had learned about the Syrian crisis and broadcast it to the student body during an assembly. The kids were thrilled to raise over $400. We saw on Twitter that our video and idea were later picked up by a high school in Illinois. They raised $800!

Be still, my world-created, unplanned-curriculum heart.

We can't always plan for this kind of curriculum, but we have an obligation to respond to it if our kids are carrying a burden of emotion. We can't plan for what a politician might say, but we can be armed with a game plan for when someone in our class is feeling uneasy as a result of tragic events they hear about beyond the classroom or hate rhetoric from the neighborhood or the world. Part of that game plan is simply the space the kids walk into each day. The best preparation to deal with these emerging topics is to have an inquiry classroom in the first place.

The physical space. Desks in clusters or tables, comfortable whole-group meeting places, rugs or carpet squares, and soft seating all send a message that this a space where kids can first be tangibly comfortable, setting their minds at ease to talk and listen to one another the way they do in the comfort of their own living rooms, playrooms, or basements.

Inquiry classrooms provide a physical space for all kids to be easily seen and heard.

Collaborative/mobile tools. Clipboards, sticky notes, maps, and tons of historical and nonfiction resources are the basic tools of inquiry, plus any technology you use as a tool to enhance the comprehension and collaboration in your classroom.

Student voice. When we allow students to have input in their own learning, we are providing them with a skill set that ranges from decision making to empathy to social action. Inquiry classrooms grow well-developed speakers and listeners. Kids are passionate about topics, teachers give them time for their passions, and the world receives learners who are driven and motivated to act because they have been empowered.

A GENERAL PLAN FOR MANAGING DISTRESSING NEWS

As I was writing this chapter, I couldn't help but reflect on the emergencies that have happened in schools where I've taught, consulted, or sent my own kids over the years. In 1988, my family's neighborhood school was the site of an early school shooting. A deranged woman named Laurie Dann, well known to the police, walked into Hubbard Woods Elementary and started firing at boys in the bathroom. My son's soccer teammate Nick Corwin died that morning. At the end of the day, Principal Dick Streedain promised the school community that he would stay at Hubbard Woods until every single child who'd been in the building that morning had gone safely on to middle school. And he did.

During my second year of teaching, I had a freshman student disclose in his dialogue journal that he was using heroin. One explicit rule of these written conversations was that if you mentioned something that could put you or someone else in danger, I reserved the right to report. I immediately sought the school social worker and the boy's counselor. These professionals swiftly got him treatment that supposedly was successful—but he never came back to school, so I was never sure.

At a downtown elementary school where I worked with teachers, there was a standing order: if an intercom announcement said, "Popcorn is now being served in the cafeteria," that meant, run your class to the east side of the building, right now! There's gunfire in the courtyard again!

At a new high school that I started with several colleagues, we had four student deaths in eight years. One was a fatal asthma attack in the school office. The others resulted from gang violence back in the kids' neighborhoods, which were scattered around many parts of Chicago. Most of our students had to be nominally gang affiliated just to get safely in and out of their home neighborhoods. When a Hispanic kid went down, his friends would make an elaborate candlelit *descanso* out of the fallen student's locker, with pictures, flowers, and farewell notes. When an African American kid was killed, the black students appropriated the Latino tradition and made the locker memorial in their own style, filled with beautiful street art and souvenirs.

With the first shooting, the faculty scrambled to set up some choices for the kids. For the time being, the class schedule was suspended. We designated a crying room for people who wanted to scream out their grief, and a quiet space for ones who felt like praying, journaling, or reflecting. Kids who just wanted to talk were invited to come to their regular advisory teacher. Other teachers posted themselves around the building, just to be present. When some of the boys got their blood up and started talking about tracking down the killers, we made a strong decision to keep them in the building. We worried that their hunger for revenge (or just to do *something*) might lead to even sadder outcomes. They were compliant (and probably relieved) when we stopped them at the stairwells. They stomped their feet and prowled in circles, cursing us: "This is bullshit man, we gotta do what we gotta do."

I'm recounting these events not to make us both sad, but to acknowledge how inescapable such emergencies are and how helpful it is to be prepared. How can we be ready?

In the previous section, Sara Ahmed reminded us of resources that inquiry teachers have at hand when unexpected news comes along—an interactive classroom setup; a culture of collaboration and problem solving; ample materials for writing, drawing, or charting; and most of all, students who are accustomed to speaking up and being listened to. But how do we know when to push further into studying a crisis and when to return to our regularly scheduled activities?

I recently spoke with a teacher who had fourteen of her students lose their homes in a sudden wildfire. These children and their classmates were utterly shocked, lost, and frightened. This was simply a catastrophe and even seasoned and loving teachers needed to avoid triggering the kids' grief—for weeks. Some child welfare organizations, like the international aid group Save the Children, think this is always the best approach. They recommend that caregivers limit themselves to listening to and comforting children. In fact, this charity cautions parents to "make sure their children's school is returning to normal patterns and not spending a lot of time discussing the disaster."

On the other hand, the National Institute of Child Health and Development (2003) recommends that students might, in a developmentally appropriate way, explore worrisome events. In one recommended activity, students look at carefully selected photos of the troubling occurrence and then draw a picture of what the world will look like when adults have fixed the situation. The American Psychological Association suggests: "Encourage your children to put their feelings into words by talking about them or journaling. Some children may find it helpful to express their feelings through art" (2011). They also say, quite wisely, "Remind [students] you are there for them to provide safety, comfort and support. Give them a hug."

So it's a tough choice. *If* a distressing event shakes your own classroom, *if* you perceive that the event is developmentally manageable, and *if* kids are asking lots of questions, you may decide to dive in. But again, which topics require more investigation and which ones should we simply leave alone, in the kids' best interests? This is where the heart and the art of a teacher come in.

If you think that further exploration of the issue will be beneficial and not deepen anxieties, then support individual, small-group, or whole-class investigations. For example, when Kristin Ziemke's first graders heard that many of the African people who lived near the lions and giraffes they had been studying had no shoes, they were shocked. They wanted to learn more about how this could happen and do something about it. Next thing you know, they mounted a shoe drive and the collected footwear went directly to Africa. As we just heard from Sara Ahmed, horrifying news about the Middle East upset her kids—but they also wanted to dig in and help. Other topics may be so shocking or worrisome that we limit ourselves to providing our students comfort and safety. For example, the next in our unending wave of public shootings might or might not be a candidate for inquiry—depending on the age of the kids, the community, the location of the event, your school's culture—and your gut.

In all this we must remember: we don't always get a chance to thoughtfully ponder the alternatives. In this hyperconnected world, neither we nor the children's parents are effective gatekeepers of the information kids are accessing. Breaking news now penetrates so deeply into our homes and our devices that we can no longer hide scary events from children, and they come to school, to us, filled with upset and juggling fragmentary information. My mentor, Neil Postman, an NYU professor and author of *The Disappearance of Childhood* (1982), warned that when a society's adults can no longer keep any secrets from its children, it will be transformed for the worse. And here we are.

When world, community, or school news is upsetting

If there is any time before you see the kids, connect with colleagues, friends, or any experts you may know. Text, call, Google. Confirm the facts as best you can. Then, when students arrive:

- Let kids know they are safe here with you, right now. Give pats and hugs as needed.
- Let children talk without interrupting. Invite everyone to speak.
- Listen carefully; be ready to hear multiple layers of concern.
- Be a calm and trustworthy adult, but not the expert with all the answers.
- Be genuine about your own feelings without telling kids how they should feel.
- Let kids know that many adults are working to help people, to fix the problem, to right the injustice, or to provide aid.
- Keep the classroom a safe space. Maintain comforting routines, return to favorite activities, revisit group friendship norms and rituals.
- Limit kids' media intake at school. Some graphic photos and videos can simply be too much for children—or for us.
- Keep your eye out for students who do not gradually bounce back, or who show significant changes in behavior, attitudes, or feelings. Promptly seek help for such children from the school psychologist, social worker, nurse, or other expert.
- Take care of yourself. You may need time, solitude, adult conversation, or just a break from the double task of managing your own emotions and supporting your students.

If an inquiry into the event seems appropriate

Now you will have at least a little prep time. First, talk with colleagues about what they are doing and collaborate to leverage the effort. Anticipating kids' wonderings, you can collect books, bookmark web pages, and gather other resources. If a story, image, poem, artifact, or literary selection will help advance kids' investigation, get it ready to use. For example, if the crisis involves street violence, you might want to read aloud *Smoky Night* by Eve Bunting. If immigration is the issue, grab *The Keeping Quilt* by Patricia Polacco. Fit these in *after* you've heard what kids want to know.

- Ask kids what they are wondering about. Jot down their questions on a public chart or let them make their own list in personal learning journals. Feel free to add items of your own or ones you hear below the surface, things kids are hesitant to express.

- As ideas are listed, confirm facts that you know; gently question rumors and misconceptions. Unless an immediate correction is required, don't say "that's wrong," but flag dubious information for double-checking later.

- If additional information or research is called for, ask: "How could we find out more about this?" Help kids develop a list of possible sources, then pursue the topic as a whole class, or subdivide the research among small groups. After a specified time, return as a whole group to share findings, and match them to the question chart made earlier.

- If kids want to take action, ask: "What are some ways we could reach out, help, or assist?" Develop a list of possible actions along a continuum of spreading awareness, taking up advocacy, or offering aid. Either as a whole class or in small teams, investigate these action options and report back to one another. When students choose an option, support them to take the necessary steps during their investigation. At this stage, finding an appropriate public outlet for students' work is one of our main roles.

- Follow up over time. Without extending the grief or upset, have check-ins where you ask, "How are we doing on _____? Anything new or old we should be talking about?" If some kids decide they want to pursue the topic longer than others, that should be OK. You just have to stay on top of their motivations and feelings, in case they become obsessive or anxious.

Sources: American Psychological Association, American School Counselors Association, National Institute of Child Health and Human Development, the National Center for School Crisis and Bereavement, the Federal Emergency Management Agency, and the Red Cross.

These jarring events provide the toughest days we face as teachers. And in case it isn't hard enough, we are always reminded to be "professional"—misguidedly meaning, "Keep your own feelings and beliefs to yourself." This policy was in full effect when I was a freshman in high school. On the day John F. Kennedy was assassinated, not one teacher said a word about it, let us talk, or changed the lesson plan. Word was passed that we could cut class if we wanted. Predictably, this abdication of adult responsibility (this inability to *deal*) led to rampant rumors, grossly magnified anxiety, and irrational fears for our own safety—in Minnesota, a thousand miles from Dallas.

In a crisis, and to be authentic to our kids, we need to tell them what we really think. It has to be OK to say, "I'm worried too" or "I feel the same way" or just plain "I don't know." We always face this kind of choice knowing we could put ourselves at odds with community or district positions. So we have to be smart. But telling the truth in the face of risk can be an opportunity for us to model what a real *upstander* does in the world.

Helpful Resources and References

American School Counselor Association. 2016. "Helping Kids During Crisis." www.schoolcounselor.org/school-counselors-members/professional -development/2016-webinar-series/learn-more/helping-kids-during-crisis.

American Psychological Association. 2011. "Helping Your Children Manage Distress in the Aftermath of a Shooting." www.apa.org/helpcenter/aftermath.aspx.

Daniels, Harvey, and Sara Ahmed. 2014. *Upstanders: Reaching Middle School Hearts and Minds with Inquiry*. Portsmouth, NH: Heinemann.

Federal Emergency Management Agency. 2016. "Children and Disasters." www .fema.gov/children-and-disasters.

National Center for School Crisis and Bereavement. 2013. "Supporting Your Students After the Death of a Family Member or Friend." www.esc3.net/cms/lib /TX00001506/Centricity/Domain/14/SupportingYourStudents2013%20AFT.pdf.

National Institute of Child Health and Human Development. 2003. *An Activity Book for African American Families: Helping Children Cope with Crisis*. NIH Pub. No. 02-5362B. www.nichd.nih.gov/publications/pubs/cope_with_crisis_book.

Postman, Neil. 1982. *The Disappearance of Childhood*. New York: Vintage.

Probst, Robert. 2010. "Difficult Days and Difficult Texts." *Voices from the Middle* 9 (2): 50–53.

Red Cross. 2004. "Helping Children Cope with Disaster." www.redcross.org /images/MEDIA_CustomProductCatalog/m14740413_Helping_children_cope _with_disaster_-_English.pdf.

Save the Children Foundation. 2017. "How to Help Children Cope with a Crisis." www.savethechildren.org/site/c.8rKLIXMGIpI4E/b.8479773/k.2264/How_to_Help _Children_Cope_with_a_Crisis.htm.

Shreve, Roberta, Karen Danbom, and Sara Hanhan. 2002. "'Wen the Flood Km We Had to Lv': Children's Understandings of Disaster." *Language Arts* 80 (2): 100–108.

Viorst, Judith. 1987. *The Tenth Good Thing About Barney.* New York: Free Press.

On the Web

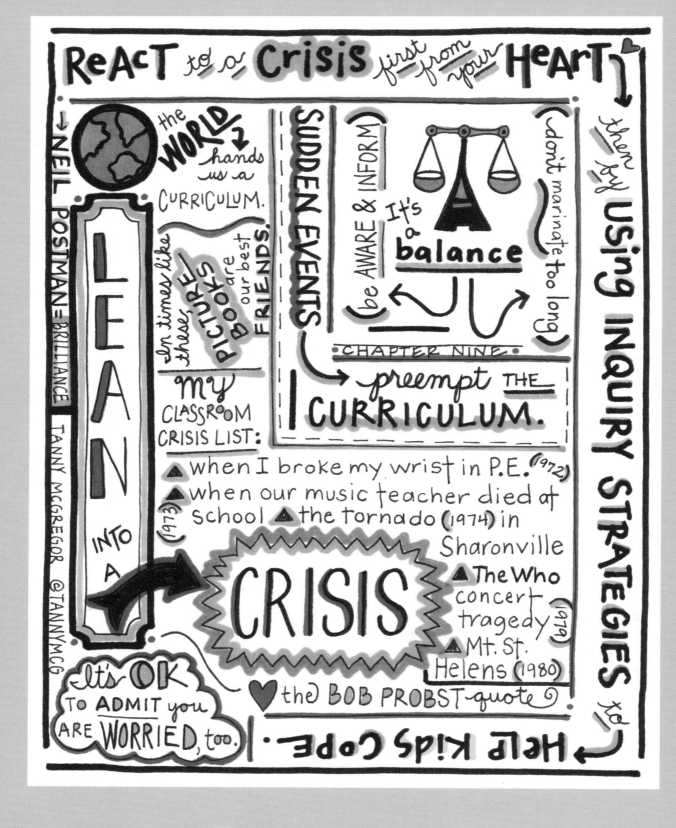

First and foremost, we need to show our human empathy and concern, and partner with the children to manage their worries. But the tools and methods of inquiry—asking questions, gathering knowledge, listening to experts, considering alternatives, and working together to plan for action— are perfectly suited to this task.

10

Learn with Partners and Pioneers

have met scores of teachers who are successfully engaging students in inquiry learning without much support from their principal, their district, or even from colleagues across the hall. These teachers often yearn for some company and some validation. But they carry on and do fantastic work with kids. They find community by following the professional literature, attending conferences, using Twitter handles and hashtags related to inquiry teaching (there are a lot!), and accessing other social media resources.

But what can interested teachers do to build more support for inquiry—right in their own classrooms, buildings, and even across a district? How can they connect, team up, plan, and coteach with colleagues? How can they seek and receive support from principals—meaning encouragement, materials, and funding for projects? How can they help spark a districtwide commitment and parental support for student-centered learning?

One way to answer these big questions is to study the pioneers—schools that have moved beyond experimenting and into wider implementation, and who have built sturdy (and replicable) supports for inquiry. Three such schools—Glenwood, Eason, and Duke—have already made their own deep, long-term commitment to student-directed inquiry. In this chapter, we'll look at some of the approaches that these schools use to foster inquiry. We'll consider both what can be done across the school (or district) to support inquiry and what you can do on your own that builds on the work these schools have pioneered.

Try This

Write down the names of the other teachers in your school. Start with your grade-level colleagues and work your way out to people you see less often. Got it? Now listen to this story.

When I was a first-year teacher, I picked out a colleague I admired and apprenticed myself to him. I needed a friend, a sounding board, a role model, and a partner. Norm Spear was a brilliant young history teacher, and we both wanted to push the envelope at our ultratraditional vocational school. By midyear, our kids were doing inquiry lessons, testifying at mock trials, and setting up historical simulations (the day of the 1929 stock market crash, how any production line compromises quality, the human geography of the Soviet Union, and more). We found an unused science lab and often brought our sixty kids together there, staging a faux purse-snatching once, among other capers. Some of our experiments were officially approved, but most we just kept secret. The point is, we drove each other to innovate and take risks every day. Truth be told, we were borderline troublemakers. We wanted kids' time at school to be worthwhile and interesting. Without each other's constant support and comradeship, those inquiry lessons, not to mention our deep relationships with kids, would have never happened.

If this story resonates with you, take a look at your list. Choose a colleague whose teaching you admire—or whose friendship you would value—and initiate a personal partnership.

If you walk into a classroom in any of these three schools today, the instruction looks so much alike that you can forget which building you are in. But this wasn't always the case. Duke School's inquiry work has its roots in its early days as Duke University's laboratory school. The founders were strongly influenced by the work of John Dewey when they set up the school in 1947. The faculty believed that children come to school with a great deal of natural curiosity, and that they learn best when teachers help them work collaboratively to explore their world and solve problems.

Since 1984 Duke School has been independent of its namesake university. As the school evolved, the faculty searched for ways to develop its inquiry-based curriculum; beginning in the early 1990s through ongoing professional development with Lilian Katz and Sylvia Chard, the school became a training institute for educators wishing to learn about the Project Approach (Katz, Chard, and Kogan 2014).

By contrast, Glenwood School has a shorter history with inquiry. In fact, in 2012–2013, the school failed to meet Wisconsin standards. Over 70 percent of the third, fourth, and fifth graders in the school were not proficient in reading on the state exam. The next year, a new leadership team was brought in with the charge to make the district something special. The school board made it clear that they didn't want the new leaders chasing test scores. They just wanted to make the district work better for kids. They were convinced that they had great teachers who were ready to move ahead. With that vote of confidence and some skillful planning, Glenwood embarked upon a continuing professional development effort built around inquiry teaching, community building, and mutual accountability among all community members.

Eason is one of eight elementary buildings in Waukee, the fastest-growing school district in Iowa. Located west of Des Moines, the district serves 9,500 students in what might have been called a rural area a few years ago. Now the once gravel road is a multilane asphalt street surrounded by new homes and businesses. In the next five years, the district plans to open its ninth elementary building, second high school, and the Waukee Innovation and Learning Center. The student population is not only growing, but also becoming increasingly diverse, with fifty-seven different languages spoken among the students in the district.

The Waukee district and the Eason Elementary community are in the sixth year of a journey toward student-directed inquiry, and they are moving fast. They are planfully shifting toward teaching from kids' questions, honoring students' curiosity, and turning over more responsibility to young people. In a community where traditional instruction might well be acceptable, and during a growth spurt that might well distract leaders from classroom innovation, Waukee teachers and leaders are pushing briskly ahead with inquiry teaching. Today, official documents use words like *passion*, *play*, *flow*, *happiness*, and even *fun* to describe the district's evolving model of optimal student learning.

These three schools might not have much in common historically, but they have something important in common in what they want for kids: at heart, they care less about mountains of data than about ensuring a warm, supportive, and engaging place for children to spend their days. In fact, this is what most parents and school board members *really* want for students, even if their concerns sometimes come across cloaked in questions about test results. When we seek support for new initiatives, we do well to keep these values, usually identical to ours, firmly in mind.

Let's see what we can learn, what can we borrow, and what we can steal from these pioneers. Hopefully, by studying their examples, we can speed up our own growth, wherever in the school world we happen to be planted.

GLENWOOD ELEMENTARY SCHOOL AND THE GREENFIELD DISTRICT

Lisa Elliott, superintendent; **Patrice Ball** and **Charity Meyer**, curriculum directors; **Steve Newcomer**, Glenwood principal; **Debra Zaffiro**, Glenwood instructional coach

When the Greenfield district failed to meet Wisconsin standards, newly appointed superintendent Lisa Elliott, curriculum directors Patrice Ball and Charity Meyer—and at Glenwood school, new principal Steve Newcomer and instructional coach Debra Zaffiro—set the wheels in motion for a transformation.

This past fall, I spent a few more days in the district, this time working with the district's fourteen new teachers (half as many as last year, a good sign of stability). By the introduction I have already given, you can probably guess who attended these sessions: the superintendent, the curriculum directors, the principals, the coaches, each new teacher's personal mentor teacher, and a school board member. Talk about putting instruction first and foremost! I asked Lisa Elliott where her own commitment comes from. She answered: "Throughout my career as a classroom teacher, I saw the power in students engaging in inquiry-based learning. Their level of engagement was high, they were excited about the learning, and there was evidence of deep understanding. Now, as the superintendent, I always consider myself as an educator, and engage in discussions, reading, and professional learning around best instructional practice. I will always be a teacher first."

POINT OUT

Most school administrators began like we did, by falling in love with children and with teaching them. So we connect with leaders through our students. We regularly invite them to observe what our kids are reading, writing, doing, making, thinking, and investigating.

Just recently, I interviewed the central office team about their approach to turning the district around four years ago. Above all, they stressed meaningful professional learning for the faculty. They felt that high-quality workshop sessions facilitated by knowledgeable presenters were part of the puzzle. But they were emphatic that teaching with inquiry is challenging work and requires job-embedded professional learning on a daily basis.

Lisa explained the next logical step. "When we met to discuss the strategy, we were all in agreement that instructional coaching was going to have the greatest impact. The staff was highly qualified and had strong pedagogical skills, and they were ready to be innovative and take the next step instructionally and wanted the support to do so."

I'm a big fan of instructional coaching myself, but I have visited schools in most states, and I can tell you: the job descriptions of coaches vary widely. Some are handed a list of "bad" teachers and ordered to fix them. Others become stealth evaluators, filling out classroom observation rubrics that affect teachers' ratings, salaries, and even their employment. Others are treated like utility infielders, subbing for sick teachers, plugging gaps, taking on different odd jobs every day. Greenfield was determined to get coaching right—so their model steered well away from these traps. The new coaches were billed as a resource to each building and its teachers, and were deployed on a "work with the willing" basis.

Some of the newly assigned coaches were found internally, but Debra Zaffiro came over from the Milwaukee Public Schools, where she had been working with Patrice Ball (and occasionally, me) on other projects. Before becoming a coach of coaches, Deb had taught in some of the city's most innovative schools. At the beginning of Chapter 7, there's a window into Deb's flexible coaching roles at Glenwood. On a spring day, she is walking past Christina Jepsen's classroom door and pauses. She sees and hears that the kindergartners have suddenly become fascinated with bees. Deb knows that bees were not on the curricular agenda for today, but she senses the energy. She makes eye contact with Christina, silently communicating, "Do you want me to help you jump on this?" Christina nods, and Deb goes upstairs to start gathering resources. Before the kids are back from lunch, Deb has delivered to Christina's room a bin of books and magazines about bees. She's rustled these up from the bookroom, from several other teachers' classroom libraries, and from her own stash of nonfiction. With this new feast of resources, the kids joyfully dig into bees for another half hour.

POINT OUT
One of the great things a coach can do is be a connector: between teachers and teachers, between teachers and resources, between kids and knowledge. If you work with a coach, is their job configured with this kind of focus and flexibility? How can you invite the coach into your work for the good of your students? How can you help them to help you? If you *are* a coach, do you need to revisit your job description with your administrator?

A key element of the Greenfield model was not just for coaches to do demonstration lessons and be resource wizards, but to get teachers into one another's classrooms. The principals had some released time funds they could use for floating subs so teachers could cross visit, observe rooms, or even coteach part of a lesson. When different faculty members saw their colleagues taking risks to explore inquiry, they were knocked out, energized, and eager to give it a try. They grew bonds of friendship much deeper than casual workroom chat could ever spark. They started seeking each other out to collaborate on projects. This strategy certainly speaks to me. In visiting hundreds of schools over the years, I have been repeatedly struck by how strong and voluntary partnerships among two or several colleagues seem to be the "secret sauce" of great teaching.

Voluntary, friendly partnerships between individual teachers are the "secret sauce" of great teaching.

POINT OUT
A good first step in getting into one another's rooms is called "teacher talk." Every time there is a faculty (or grade-level) meeting, it is scheduled in a different teacher's classroom. For the first fifteen minutes of the session, the owner of the room explains to colleagues why the room is set up as it is, what the functional areas of the room are, and how teaching resources are displayed and used. After some questions and discussion, the meeting proceeds with its main agenda.

It's fun to watch Steve Newcomer being a principal, roaming around the building, coffee cup perennially in hand. He's constantly present, in and out of classrooms, greeting kids by name, having mini consultations with eager students who grab him in the hall. Steve taught for eighteen years before becoming an administrator, and his teacher chops are obvious when he works with kids.

In his first year as principal, when the district was making the transition toward student-directed inquiry, Steve knew that some of the teachers were doubtful or even fearful of this new pedagogy. So, for the next staff meeting at Glenwood, Steve assembled three short video clips for the teachers to watch. He offered no commentary and simply asked the faculty to guess what the message was. (If you want to re-create that workshop for yourself, just watch the first minute and a half of each one.) The three clips were:

1. A Jimmy Fallon episode in which Idina Menzel sings "Let It Go" from the *Frozen* movie soundtrack, accompanied by Jimmy's house band, the Roots, playing schoolroom instruments.

    www.youtube.com/watch?v=17QQcK4l6Yw

2. A video montage of people doing incredibly daring things like helicopter-in snowboarding, cliff diving, and base jumping.

    www.youtube.com/watch?v=mFThmi1RV3I

3. The music video of Pharrell Williams singing "Happy."

    www.youtube.com/watch?v=y6Sxv-sUYtM&list=PLlmeWccdlw Pl5HrbQz7XaMrEMi4V8cDtC

After some sing-alongs, whoas, and laughs, teachers had figured out Steve's three-part message for the new school year:

Let your fears go.

Take some risks.

Have fun.

POINT
OUT

When I visit highly successful schools, there are certain attributes I almost always see. One is genuine friendship and personal relationships among the staff. Another is a smart, approachable principal who is a keeper of the vision, but who is also fully part of that friendship network. If that's your situation, make friends with your principal.

If Steve's video workshop seems a little unusual, let's reframe it as an example of principalship. In the research on school leadership, there are five sources of authority:

1. Ability to punish
2. Ability to reward
3. Position of authority
4. Expertise
5. Friendship

Only the last two can be linked to increased student achievement (Schmuck and Schmuck 2000). This profound understanding informs all of the moves that Glenwood School has been making for the last four years, during which it moved from probation to meeting state standards to "exceeds expectations"

EASON ELEMENTARY SCHOOL AND THE WAUKEE SCHOOL DISTRICT

Ali Locker and Lindsay Law, directors of teaching and learning; **Clint Prohaska**, principal; **Stacy Hansen**, teacher

Eason Elementary opened in 1994 as a K–2 building. It was the second elementary in the Waukee School District and was located on a gravel road east of town. Over the past twenty-two years, that country road has become one of the busiest streets in the Waukee area and is surrounded by homes and businesses. Eason is currently made up of 580 students in kindergarten through fifth grade and each student is a unique, valued member of the culture. Teachers believe that every child has the ability to impact the world in a distinctive, positive way by posing their own questions, exercising their passions, and finding their purpose.

Clint Prohaska, Principal

Over the past five years I have been blessed to work at Eason Elementary as a fifth-grade teacher, assistant principal, and currently as the principal. During this time I have seen a major shift take place as teachers have evolved toward more inquiry-based instruction. This change began when the prior principal, Peg Erke, took a group of teachers to a Heinemann Inquiry Institute in New Orleans five years ago. When they returned, they started exploring ways that our students could share their curiosities, learn multiple reading and writing strategies, and "go public" with new learning by sharing their findings with peers. We spent the next couple of years learning more about the inquiry process as a staff, with book studies, with our own experiments, and at professional development institutes. We used the book *Comprehension and Collaboration: Inquiry Circles for Curiosity, Engagement, and Understanding* (Harvey and Daniels 2015) as one guide, and encouraged more teachers to experiment with the inquiry process to connect social studies and science content with reading and writing standards. We gave teachers opportunities to reflect on their students' learning experience, supported teacher study groups, and sent more teachers to the Santa Fe and New Orleans Inquiry Institutes.

After studying inquiry-based instruction and experimenting with it in the classroom, we were ready for the next step. We decided that we had to live the process from a student's point of view to better understand how our students feel when experiencing inquiry learning. We used our professional development time to create our own inquiries about the history and future of our school and district. We posed questions about our own interests, teamed up with colleagues with similar curiosities, researched and interviewed people around the town, and shared our learning with our colleagues. This experience helped us to personally grasp the excitement and challenge that inquiry can have on learners.

Since that time, inquiry has become a way of life. We don't "do" inquiry; we *live it* every day. We practice inquiry on a daily basis in our classrooms,

We don't "do" inquiry; we *live it* every day.

committee meetings, professional learning opportunities, and interactions among each other. We don't always follow a formal inquiry process, but we constantly look for ways to acknowledge curiosities, enhance thinking, and give students opportunities to share their new learning. Of course, we will continue to change and evolve the way we approach teaching as our students need us to. But we will always live with inquiring minds, focused on what our students need to fulfill themselves and make the world a better place.

Stacy Hansen, Fifth-Grade Teacher

As a teacher, how do you work with your administrators? Invite them into your classroom! Not just to observe, but to learn and coteach alongside you. Involve them in your visions and hopes for students. Share your stories of success beyond quantitative data. Ground yourself in the purpose of the work you are doing with students and be willing to share celebrations and failures with colleagues. Approach leadership with solutions, not problems.

I have always considered myself lucky to work in a district with an administration that supports teachers who are innovative and want to try new ideas in their classroom. As I reflect about where that support comes from, I think it is built around a mutual respect between teachers and administrators and the belief that exploring new ideas can lead to growth for both teachers and students. When I am brainstorming ways to engage my students, I try to define my purpose (my "why") and justify why the chosen approach might work. I expect and welcome questions from administration, but I also hope to encounter an open mind. If what I am doing requires a substantial shift, I go to my administrator early in the process rather than springing it on them as I am implementing my ideas.

After I establish my "why," my students get to develop the "how." Most often, when administrators hear about a new idea I want to try, they are just as excited as I am about it. I invite them in to see the idea in action—or to try it out themselves—because we adults need to stay curious and take risks too. Support from my administration comes from the fact that I've thought my idea through, am focused on meeting learning objectives, and have determined that this approach will work for my kids. I appreciate support when I have the opportunity to try new things even if I don't know exactly where it will lead. Even when these experiments initially seem unsuccessful, they often yield a host of unforeseen lessons which can lead me to something better than the original plan.

Ali Locker and Lindsay Law, directors of Teaching and Learning

You cannot help but believe in inquiry. When you enter learning through the eyes of a student, you know that curiosity, wonder, passion, and play are the gateway to constructing true meaning and deep understanding. Planning and preparation carry a different momentum, a motivation that reciprocates the kids' engagement. The evidence of effectiveness is visible and present, so believing in inquiry parallels living it. The energy, eagerness, and enthusiasm of kids' learning is lively. The mind-set around learning becomes a collective efficacy among students and teachers in the classroom. Students become emotionally invested in their learning. It makes everyone that much more invested. Learning becomes more accessible and functional for students through inquiry. As a teacher, you get to be the architect of that instructional design. You get to create the opportunities for them to explore.

Each day of inquiry work gives us momentum toward new information, a new perspective, a new truth to discover from the world. But we had to get used to letting go of control. The trade-off was always worth it, especially when we saw reluctant readers digging through text to find answers to their own burning questions—rather than "completing the task" of answering mine. In truth, inquiry is as liberating for the teachers as the students: it was easier to plan when we could approach the material from the perspective of a learner.

Student-driven inquiry ignites a spirit of learning in children. Interactions among classmates increase, students' time in text improves, students' conversations and use of vocabulary have depth, and the classroom has a new chemistry. Students take their inquiry right into recess, their lunchtime conversations, and their homes. By spring, they are making connections to concepts from early fall. Once immersed in inquiry, you will find yourself wondering why you were not "all in" from the start.

Once we had seen increases in student engagement, motivation, and achievement in several classrooms across the district, we were eager to share this work on a larger scale. Our inquiry map draws from what we saw in successful classrooms. Today it is our district's approach for teaching and learning.

The curriculum map [Figure 10.1] is not meant as an entry-point teaching tool for how to make inquiry work in a single classroom. It is intended to be a universal and conceptual guide to the way we operate as a district.

POINT OUT

Eason's curriculum map is bold and inspiring (to me anyway) and deliciously idiosyncratic. It vibrantly speaks the values of those educators in that place. But yours would be different, if you sat down with your own colleagues and started noodling about how you really want learning to feel in your building or district. So, grab some fellow teachers and some markers and dream big.

Our parents and community have been a huge part of our growth toward a curiosity-driven curriculum. We found that the best way to bring parents along with innovative teaching methods like inquiry was to model our efforts in the same way that students do when "going live and public." A newsletter or informational meeting was just not going to cut it. We found ways to use music, art, and technology to share our vision of inquiry in a really "live" way—with video.

On the Web

Videos from Waukee

Rockstar: www.youtube.com/watch?v=EwGQONGyio4

Heart of Waukee: www.youtube.com/watch?v=5yUFRlwLhKY

Fifth-Grade Dance Party: https://www.youtube.com/watch?v=sBHZm2EHSVg
You can also find the links to these videos on our website: hein.pub/CuriousClassroom.

On this book's website are links to some inspiring videos that the Waukee Schools created to educate parents and community members about their evolving inquiry-based curriculum. As the refrain of one of the songs says, "At Waukee we wonder all the time." Check them out.

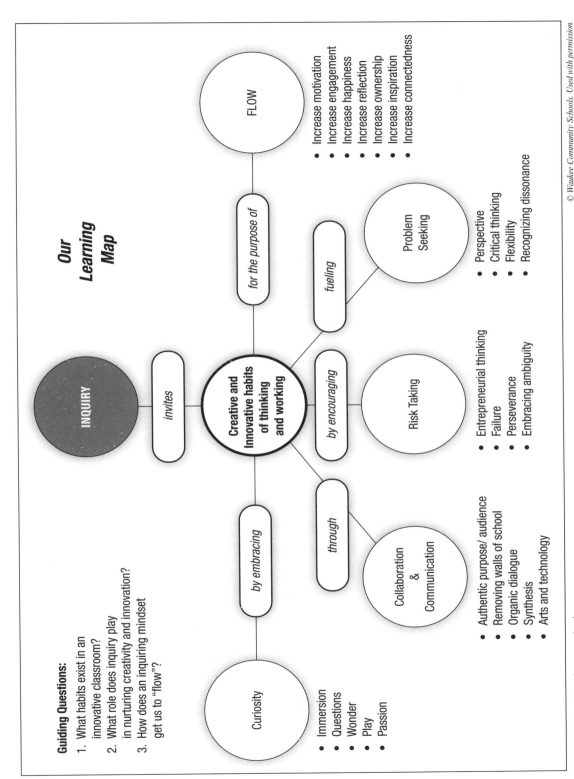

Guiding Questions:

1. What habits exist in an innovative classroom?
2. What role does inquiry play in nurturing creativity and innovation?
3. How does an inquiring mindset get us to "flow"?

Our Learning Map

INQUIRY

invites

Creative and Innovative habits of thinking and working

for the purpose of

FLOW

- Increase motivation
- Increase engagement
- Increase happiness
- Increase reflection
- Increase ownership
- Increase inspiration
- Increase connectedness

fueling

Problem Seeking

- Perspective
- Critical thinking
- Flexibility
- Recognizing dissonance

by encouraging

Risk Taking

- Entrepreneurial thinking
- Failure
- Perseverance
- Embracing ambiguity

through

Collaboration & Communication

- Authentic purpose/ audience
- Removing walls of school
- Organic dialogue
- Synthesis
- Arts and technology

by embracing

Curiosity

- Immersion
- Questions
- Wonder
- Play
- Passion

Figure 10.1 Waukee curriculum map

DUKE SCHOOL

Kathy Bartlemay, curriculum director, and **Jenny Murray**, middle school director

Two core beliefs have enabled Duke School to continue its inquiry-based projects over the decades. First is the clear understanding by board members, administrators, and teachers that the school's primary mission is to prepare the next generation of problem solvers for our complex world. To accomplish this, all classes engage in three six- to eight-week projects, often curriculum based, per year. Through this work, students are taught the process of exploring and observing their world, asking deep questions, conducting investigations, and working collaboratively to share their findings with a larger audience. On any given day, one might see kindergarten children, clipboards in hand, interviewing a veterinarian about ways to take care of pets. Meanwhile, three fifth graders are creating a video for Habitat for Humanity as they culminate research for their project Reaching Out: Agencies That Support Our Community. Throughout its history, Duke School has remained relentlessly focused on inquiry-based project work at all levels.

The second core belief is that great inquiry work doesn't happen overnight. It grows and develops over time. In the same manner that our students conduct inquiries, teachers and administrators keep track of their own questions and wonderings, meet regularly to do research and share ideas, and invite "guest experts" to campus to help us. Just a few years ago the upper elementary and middle school teachers expressed concerns that student project work was not as deep as it might be. To address these concerns, we launched a book study and brought in experts in the field. Our faculty continue to pose questions, collaborate, and revise their teaching.

How We Support Project-Based Learning and Inquiry Work

1. *Administrators know and actively study pedagogy.* At Duke School, the division directors and curriculum director attend workshops alongside teachers. They participate in project planning and evaluation meetings. They visit classrooms frequently and engage in conversations with students. They help ensure that all classrooms in the school have a common process and language.

2. *We hire with inquiry work in mind.* When adding to our faculty, we place a high priority on experience in promoting student inquiry. In interviews, Duke School looks for teachers who value student questioning and investigating, who actively engage students in discourse and collaboration, and who are open to collaborating with other faculty members.

3. *Class schedules dedicate time to inquiry work.* Teachers create schedules with blocks of time for inquiry-based project work, along with blocks for traditional content areas. Curriculum maps are crafted so that informational reading and writing units during our workshop blocks support the investigations students do during their project block.

4. *Teachers have collaborative planning time.* Simply said, teachers must have time to plan together for integrated inquiry projects to be successful. Special classes such as PE and art are scheduled back to back so that the grade-level team can have planning time. Additional planning time occurs once each week as administrators or parent volunteers cover lunch and recess duty for grade-level teams. In this way, our whole community honors and values the need for adults to work together to meet our curricular goals.

If you don't have the planning time you need to collaborate with your colleagues, make an inquiry project out of it. Together, study your weekly schedule and see if you can spot a window for teacher planning time—and then propose it to your principal.

POINT OUT

5. *We've created touchstone projects.* With our long history of inquiry-based project work, Duke School teachers have developed an inventory of project topics and plans. While many large ideas and researchable questions are repeated each year in these project topics, others are not, as teachers follow the needs and interests of each particular group of children. Having project topics that can be repeated allows teachers to gather appropriate resources, readable texts, and guest experts, as well as develop their own expertise to be better able to guide students as they search for answers and draw conclusions. Students still take

ownership of asking individual questions, researching answers, and sharing newly gained expertise with others, and therefore their final products and culminating experiences reflect the learning and individuality of that year's class.

Remember that Duke has been doing inquiry for seventy years! The takeaway for most of us is to save our projects, along with their materials, plans, and samples of student work, so we can share or repeat them in the future.

6. *We've recruited a bank of local experts.* One cornerstone of our project work has always been to bring primary research into the classroom by using adult professional experts. Students learn to ask questions and develop interview skills while gaining knowledge from people with specific expertise. We are fortunate to be located near several major universities, but our experts also come from the local community and parent body. Teachers might call on a dentist for a Healthy Self project or an anthropologist to Skype about a new humanoid species discovery. Often our relationship with visiting experts begins when a parent of a child in the class has an area of expertise or a talent that is related to a current class project. After the experience, though, many experts return year after year, even after their child has graduated.

On pages 109–110, Duke teacher Carolynn Klein Hageman shares a handout on how to find and use classroom experts, which is a great tool for getting started.

7. *Process documentation.* Ongoing documentation of learning and the inquiry process is a defining feature of our work. In the younger grades, teachers document the process for the students, while in upper elementary and middle school, teachers and students partner to create displays that track classroom activities, field experiences, thinking, questioning, and learning. This documentation serves two main

purposes. One, students can see, assess, and reflect on what they've been doing. It's easy to refer back to an early learning activity as they learn new information and draw conclusions from the sum of their experiences, questioning further and deepening their understanding. Second, we document to communicate with and educate our parent body. When students share their final products and projects during our culminating events, parents may not initially see and understand how the students got to that place in their learning. By sharing the entire process, parents begin to understand and value process over product.

The degree to which Duke has refined its inquiry work is impressive, but it's helpful to remember that the work they're doing today was built on constant improvement over many years and many attempts. In your own inquiry work, or in inquiry work across the school, make it a priority to name your processes, as in Figures 10.2 and 10.3. Then, see how and when it makes sense to align processes on a larger scale, and revisit these processes each time you use them.

POINT OUT

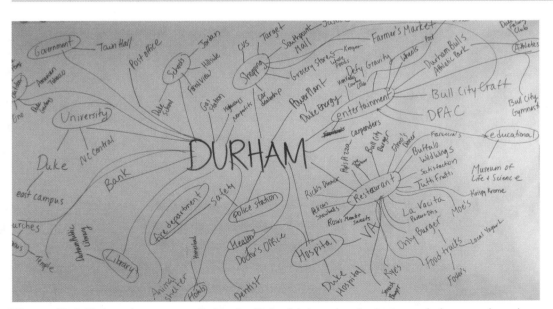

Figure 10.2 To launch a community inquiry, Duke third graders brainstormed places and services around town that they were familiar with.

8. *Common features, language, and documents.* Some institutionalized features of project work can be quite simple, yet still bring large dividends in consistency of structure. At Duke, we have developed planning documents for each project. Documentation includes key features such as accessing what students already know,

> # PHASE ONE: WEB
> WE LAUNCHED OUR DURHAM PROJECT BY CREATING A WEB OF SOME THINGS WE ALREADY KNOW ABOUT OUR COMMUNITY.
> STUDENTS CONSIDERED TWO QUESTIONS:
> 1: WHAT ARE YOUR FAVORITE PLACES IN DURHAM?
> 2: WHAT SERVICES ARE IMPORTANT IN KEEPING OUR COMMUNITY SAFE AND RUNNING SMOOTHLY?

Figure 10.3 As they moved along in their research, kids and their teachers named and documented each stage of the inquiry.

guiding students to ask and revise questions, and conducting group and individual research. On the planning form, teachers record enduring understandings and essential questions, as well as skills and strategies in literacy, research, and other content areas. Although these documents are adjusted every year, common language, learning outcomes, and big ideas are never lost.

9. *A culture of sharing and learning from each other.* Collaboration and learning from colleagues is important for students and teachers alike. At Duke School, we share all phases of our inquiry project work during teacher study groups and faculty meetings as well as visits to one another's culminating events. Throughout this process, teachers learn from each other, offer suggestions, ask questions, and share resources and knowledge. By creating a culture of learning from each other, we model and live the collaborative nature of inquiry work. It's also fun and helpful!

10. *Reflection, evaluation, and goal setting.* In addition to sharing and learning from each other while we're working on projects, we reflect on and evaluate our projects in a dedicated meeting after each project's completion. While the project is still fresh in their minds, teachers meet with the curriculum director and division director to discuss what went well and what they might change in the future. We use a school-created rubric to assess project features such as curricular objectives, real-world

connections, diversity components, student work and assessments, and the culminating event. These conversations are rich as they allow teachers and administrators to reflect and set goals for individuals, teaching teams, or the school as a whole. In this way, we all continue to inform not only our teaching, but also our learning.

There are many plenty of takeaways from the pioneer teachers and pathfinding schools that have developed their inquiry work over years or decades.

- Get others into your classroom and get yourself into theirs.
- Reach out to your colleagues, and start doing small projects together.
- Make friends with your principal through your kids and their work.
- Take advantage of district PD; if it's not valuable, ask for what you need.
- If you have a coach, bond with her or him.
- As Steve Newcomer recommends: let it go, take a risk, and have fun.

Final Thoughts

I've spent the last couple hundred pages trying to show how wonderful inquiry learning can be for so many kids. I've presented you with research, teachers' stories, kids' writing, posters, charts, photographs, and even classroom videos. I hope you're convinced that, as we say in the trade, "this stuff works" for students.

But here's the other not-so-secret benefit: inquiry is also better for *us*, the teachers. Not to be selfish, but we deserve to have some pleasure in the classroom too. Nobody talks about *teacher* engagement, but after ten years of standards, testing, accountability, and scripted curricula, we are at risk for "dropping out" ourselves—mentally if not physically. School should be *fun* for teachers, just as it should be for students. And when we step off stage and become research partners with our students, that's when the real fun begins for us.

Last year, I decided to hang around exclusively in classrooms where student-directed inquiry was emerging. And I know so much more now: I have delighted in learning about tornadoes, eagles, Pluto, composting, insider trading, Flamin' Hot

Cheetos, terrible feet, baked Alaska, identity, empathy, peanut butter diamonds, the importance of play, Throwback Thursdays, Travel Tuesdays, theatre management, Inky the octopus, meteorology, Facing History and Ourselves, crazy state laws, DIY gymnasium games, and how to cope with frightening life events.

Spending time with all these amazing kids and teachers has made me a much smarter and more optimistic person. I hope your explorations in inquiry do the same for you—and all your students. Curiosity rocks!

Curiosity, collaboration, and discovery are the heartbeat of inquiry.

Works Cited

Allen, Thomas J., and Jeffrey W. Sherman. 2011. "Ego Threat and Intergroup Bias: A Test of Motivated-Activation Versus Self-Regulatory Accounts." *Psychological Science* 22 (3): 331–333. DOI:10.1177/0956797611399291.

Beane, James. 2006. *A Reason to Teach. Creating Classrooms of Dignity and Hope*. Portsmouth, NH: Heinemann.

Beckoff, Mark. 2007. *The Emotional Lives of Animals*. Novato, CA: New World Library.

Beeler, Carolyn. 2016. "Inky the Octopus Escapes New Zealand Aquarium, Makes It to Ocean." *USA Today*. April 14.

Buck Institute. 2016. "Why Project Based Learning?" https://www.bie.org/about/why_pbl.

Calkins, Lucy. *Units of Study for Teaching Reading*. Portsmouth, NH: Heinemann.

Calkins, Lucy. *Units of Study for Teaching Writing*. Portsmouth, NH: Heinemann.

Daniels, Harvey, and Sara Ahmed. 2015. *Upstanders: How to Engage Middle School Hearts and Minds with Inquiry*. Portsmouth, NH: Heinemann.

Daniels, Harvey, and Nancy Steineke. 2014. *Teaching the Social Skills of Academic Interaction*. Thousand Oaks, CA: Corwin.

Daniels, Harvey, and Steven Zemelman. 2014. *Subjects Matter*. 2nd ed. Portsmouth, NH: Heinemann.

Expeditionary Learning. 2015. "Our Approach." http://eleducation.org/about/our-approach.

Gallagher, Kelly. 2016. "Article of the Week." Building Deeper Readers & Writers. www.kellygallagher.org/article-of-the-week.

Gray, Peter. 2013. *Free to Learn*. New York: Basic Books.

Harvey, Stephanie, and Harvey Daniels. 2015. *Comprehension and Collaboration: Inquiry Circles for Curiosity, Engagement, and Understanding*. Revised ed. Portsmouth, NH: Heinemann.

Katz, Lilian, Sylvia Chard, and Yvonne Kogan. 2014. *Engaging Children's Minds: The Project Approach*. 3rd ed. Santa Barbara, CA: Praeger.

Kessler, Chris. 2013. "What Is Genius Hour?" www.geniushour.com/what-is-genius-hour.

MacPherson, Erin. 2016. "STEM: It's Elementary." www.weareteachers.com/blogs/post/2015/04/03/stem-its-elementary.

Muhtaris, Katie, and Kristin Ziemke. 2015. *Amplify: Digital Teaching and Learning in the K–6 Classroom*. Portsmouth, NH: Heinemann.

Paul, Anne Murphy. 2013. "How to Stimulate Curiosity." NPR/KQED. April 8. https://ww2.kqed.org/mindshift/2013/04/08/how-to-stimulate-curiosity/.

Pink, Daniel. 2009. *Drive: The Surprising Truth About What Motivates Us*. New York: Riverhead.

Responsive Classroom. 2016. *The Joyful Classroom: Practical Ways to Engage and Challenge Students K–6*. Turners Falls, MA: Center for Responsive Schools.

Schmuck, Richard, and Patricia Schmuck. 2000. *Group Processes in the Classroom*. New York: McGraw Hill.

Seppala, Emma. 2016. *The Happiness Track*. New York: HarperCollins.

Steineke, Nancy. 2009. *Assessment Live: 10 Real-Time Ways for Kids to Show What They Know—and Meet the Standards.* Portsmouth NH: Heinemann.

Strauss, Valerie. 2012. "$1.1 Million-Plus Gates Grants: 'Galvanic' Bracelets That Measure Student Engagement." *Washington Post*. June 12.

"Unusual Laws." OnlyintheStateofTexas.com. www.onlyinthestateoftexas.com/laws.html.

Wormeli, Rick. 2015. "Calling for a 'Timeout' on Rubrics and Grading Scales." *AMLE Magazine* 4 (3): 41–43. www.amle.org/BrowsebyTopic/WhatsNew/WNDet/TabId/270/ArtMID/888/ArticleID/539/Rubrics-and-Grading-Scales.aspx.

Zaslow, Stephanie. 2016. "5th-Graders Form Sign Language Club to Communicate with Deaf Classmate." *Today Show.* March 2. www.today.com/health/5th-graders-form-sign-language-club-communicate-deaf-classmate-t77386.

Zemelman, Steven, Harvey Daniels, and Arthur Hyde. 2012. *Best Practice: Bringing Standards to Life in America's Schools*. 4th ed. Portsmouth, NH: Heinemann.